W9-AQU-328

JAN 1988

RECEIVED
OHIO DOMINICAN
COLLEGE LIBRARY
COLUMBUS, OHIO
43219

31-1234567891011121314151617181920212223242526272829303

Hadi Khorsandi is Iran's best known comic talent. His early satire, sharp but apolitical under the Shah, was radicalised by the Iranian Revolution of 1979, sparing neither the mullahs nor their opponents.

This collection of Khorsandi's recent post-revolutionary writing highlights a genial and inventive spirit that will be instantly attractive to readers everywhere. Khorsandi's humorous essays and flawless parodies of the mullahs' pronouncements, sermons, war strategies, interviews with a servile press—taken from his émigré magazine *Asghar Agha*—all give fresh insights on the veil, the war and Irangate.

Hadi Khorsandi

THE AYATOLLAH
AND I

translated by Ehssan Javan

readers international

891.557
K45a
1987

These pieces appeared in Persian in the journal *Asghar Agha*, published in London by the author, between 1979 and 1987.

Copyright © Hadi Khorsandi 1987

First published in English by Readers International Inc., New York, and Readers International, London. Editorial inquiries to London office at 8 Strathray Gardens, London NW3 4NY, England. US/Canadian inquiries to Subscriber Service Department, P.O. Box 959, Columbia, Louisiana 71418-0959, USA.

English translation copyright © Readers International Inc. 1987
All rights reserved

Cover Art and design by an Iranian artist
Typesetting by Grassroots Typeset, London N3
Printed and bound in Great Britain

ISBN 0-930523-36-9 Hardcover
ISBN 0-930523-37-7 Paperback

About the translator: **Ehssan Javan** is the pseudonym of a London-based expert on Iranian affairs.

Introduction

Several dozen periodicals are published by Iranians in exile, representing a wide range of opinion, from support for the restoration of the monarchy to various strands of socialism. What most of these journals have in common is that their readership is mainly those sharing their own political views. An outstanding exception is the magazine *Asghar Agha*, published in London for the past eight years by the veteran Iranian satirist Hadi Khorsandi.

Born in the provincial town of Fariman, Khorsandi began his career with the satirical weekly *Towfiq* when he was still a high school student. By the mid-seventies, Khorsandi was one of Iran's most successful journalists, writing a regular column for one of the country's two main dailies, *Ettela'at* (Information), and for the weekly, *Zan-e Rouz* (Modern Woman). He also wrote scripts for radio, television and nightclub comedy shows. Written under the watchful eyes of the Shah's censor, it was inevitable that most of Khorsandi's satire, like all other published or performed work, had to be more or less "tame". None the less, in a country where many buy newspapers merely to read the death notices—traditionally regarded as the only truthful items—Khorsandi's *Ettela'at* column boosted the newspaper's circulation in no small measure. On more than

126586

one occasion the column appeared blank, except for Khorsandi's byline and photograph, indicating that the censor, rather than a negligent printer, had intervened.

In December 1978, while in London, he wrote a satirical poem criticising the Shah and his regime and praising Ayatollah Khomeini, his words immediately becoming part of Iran's revolutionary repertoire. But Ayatollah Khomeini's regime proved even less tolerant of Khorsandi's satire than its predecessor. Some of his critical poems and articles, published in Iranian newspapers after his return to Iran led to protests by Hezbollahi (Party of Allah) mobs who eventually demanded his execution. Heart-broken and fearing for his life, Khorsandi flew back to London on 3 April 1979, only two days after the official proclamation of an Islamic Republic in Iran.

In London, he has so far published over 250 issues of a journal he first called *Taghoot* (Idol), a term used by Ayatollah Khomeini and the Islamic Republic to describe not only the Shah and his regime, but also all aspects of life which do not conform to their dogmatic outlook. The magazine was retitled *Asghar Agha*, the name of a fictitious character developed by Khorsandi in his *Ettela'at* column, in order not to scare away potential readers among Iranian tourists visiting London.

An unsuccessful plot to assassinate Khorsandi, uncovered by Scotland Yard in May 1984, has meant that the editor/publisher must continue to keep a low profile, even in exile.

Over the years, Khorsandi has become disillusioned with much of the organised opposition abroad to Ayatollah

Khomeini's regime, be they monarchists, Islamic guerrillas, Mojahedin-e Khalq, or the numerous leftist groups and factions. And as promises on all sides for a quick overthrow of the Islamic regime in Tehran fail to bear fruit, his newspaper, which pokes fun at opposition as well as at the regime, has gained more and more readers in Iranian communities all over the world.

There are contributions to the paper from other Iranian writers and artists, but by and large the work is that of Khorsandi himself, writing in a number of styles, verse and prose. In addition to the fictitious Asghar Agha, who features in the paper as the voice of common sense speaking on behalf of the man in the street, Khorsandi has created other characters, chief among whom is Sadeq Sedaqat, literally meaning "Truthful Truthfulness". This character, whom Khorsandi describes as "a simple youth who knows nothing about anything", is introduced by Iranian high school-style "essays". These "essays", collected and published in Persian in London in 1983, can be read as Khorsandi's personal, and at times emotional, account of post-revolutionary developments in Iran. Khorsandi has also published another collection of articles, entitled *Friday Prayers Sermons,* written in the style of Ayatollah Khomeini's speeches. Sometimes one has to examine these carefully to be sure they are not the genuine article.

—The Translator

Note to My English-Language Readers

My travel document says I can travel anywhere in the world, except to my own country. While we exiled Iranians are forbidden to return to our homeland, every week the McFarlanes, the Farlanovs, the Farlanssons, the de Farlaines and all types of other wheeler-dealer, profiteering Farlanes from China, Japan, Western and Eastern Europe can land at Tehran airport. And only rarely does someone blow the whistle on them.

Some ten years now I have been searching for news about my lost homeland in the crackling short-waves of the radio and among the pages of the old newspapers that arrive from Iran. Meanwhile, Lt-Col Oliver North's personal secretary, Fawn, has had continuous access to the hottest and most recent news direct from my country.

My country has been hijacked, with more than 40 million people on board. Not a day passes without the hijackers throwing the bodies of hundreds of young passengers out the emergency exits into the marshes along the Iraqi border. Do Messrs Reagan and Gorbachev, when they meet in their well-publicised summits, spare a thought for the Iranian and Iraqi youths killed daily in the war? And do they even suppose that between the Caspian Sea and the Persian Gulf there lives a people who want their country to be free and independent?

We Iranians differentiate between a people and their blind-hearted leaders. We ask you likewise to distinguish between the Iranian people and the regime that misleads us. I hope that the publication of part of my work in English will enable the freedom-loving people of the world to learn more about the fresh wounds inflicted on an old nation; to appreciate their responsibilities with respect to the situation in which we find ourselves; and to react in a manner befitting them and us.

Hadi Khorsandi
London, May 1987

Contents

THE AYATOLLAH AND I

PART ONE

IN WHICH Mr President
Dr Bani-Sadr
is completely surrounded
by worries...
(1979 to 1981)

Fable

And during the war, there was this mullah who had bought a truck-load of foodstuffs was carrying it home. "Why are you doing that?" he was asked. "Haven't you heard," he replied, "that the counter-revolutionaries are hoarding foodstuffs in order to create a fictitious shortage? Well, I'm going to hide this so well that no counter-revolutionary will ever find it."

5 October 1980

The President's Diary—1*

I wake up at 11 a.m., I mean the Revolutionary Guards inside the bunker wake me up and tell me it's time we retreated because the Iraqis are advancing. Looks like we have to pull back a couple of miles before we can get on with our sleep.

Word comes from Tehran that, for the time being, our speeches ought to include the words "Iran" and "the Nation" more frequently, but not more than four times in any one speech, for we should make sure that Islam gets all the credit. Feeling thirsty, I reach for a bottle, but the soldier jumps up and grabs it from me, saying I shouldn't drink from it because it's a Molotov cocktail. I tell them to punish the bastard Molotov so he doesn't leave his cocktail bottle in our bunker again.

I turn on the radio and hear the news that the head of radio and television has been changed and the Imam has appointed one of his own mullahs in his place. Goodness me! Once again the Imam has taken advantage of my

* "The President's Diary" draws on Dr Bani-Sadr's own column published in his newspaper, *The Islamic Revolution*, in Iran, under the title "How the Days Pass before the President". (Translator's note)

absence. But between ourselves, our presence or absence is the same for the Imam. In the end he does whatever he wants to do. I pick up the binoculars and take a look at the Shatt-al-Arab. I see that the Iraqi forces have taken both banks of the river and one can't even bathe. I've brought along my loin-cloth and towel for nothing.

A Revolutionary Guard comes along, gives me his rifle and tells me to have a go at the enemy while he's out at the latrine. Being the Commander-in-Chief, I decide I shouldn't dodge. But I would have been much happier to go to the toilet instead of that Revolutionary Guard's and not to hold this gun in my hand. The damned thing is so heavy too. And it has a very strange shape. You can't tell which end of it you should shoot the enemy with. I hold the gun ready and wait for the enemy. A couple of hours pass but the enemy doesn't turn up. The Revolutionary Guard doesn't turn up either. Now the enemy might have chickened out, but why should a Revolutionary Guard take so long at the toilet? And in war time too. I mean, should a Revolutionary Guard's stomach be in such a bad state?

I wait until dusk, but there is no sign either of the enemy or of the Revolutionary Guard. I radio to say I am all alone on the front line. But they tell me to come off it, because this is not really the front line, but just a bunker they have made up as a "VIP Lounge", so that when the leaders of the Revolution want to join the battle or when the Imam's grandson Hossein wants to fight for Islam, they'd have somewhere to go to hold guns in their hands and pose for pictures.

We see that we've been conned and have wasted our

16

time; otherwise, in these same few hours we could have inflicted lots of damage on the enemy. These people from the Army have really gone too far. They have kept all the real bunkers for themselves and have given all the fake, safe and useless ones to the Revolutionary Guards, the militant clergy and the Iranian Nation's gallant President. I drop the gun and wave for a helicoper to take us straight to Tehran. Pakistan's Zia ul-Haq has arrived to talk about peace. The Imam's son Ahmad comes over immediately with his father's message that we should not utter a word about peace.

"Hey," I want to know, "how many Commanders-in-Chief have we got?".

"Just one."

5 October 1980

How to run Basra

In Baghdad President Saddam Hossein has put out a "dead or alive" reward for General Oveissi of the Shah's Army, said to have encouraged the Iraqi leader to invade Iran. Saddam Hossein has never been in such a mess.

Now Iran has set four conditions for letting Iraq off the hook. One of these is that Iraq should hand over its port of Basra to Iran. It might well be easy to take Basra from Iraq, but will it be as easy to run the city? Of course not. Before taking delivery of Basra from Iraq, we must have access to a detailed map of the city and put crosses on it here and there to mark the various parts where Islamic Revolutionary Committees are to be set up, because a town without *Komitehs* is good for nothing.

If there are any universities in Basra, we must close them down as soon as possible. Furthermore, now that we have an opportunity to export our revolution to Basra, have we provided enough whips for all the people of the city? I mean, really, you can't export a revolution without whips. In my opinion, within minutes of capturing Basra and raising the Islamic Republic's flag on its buildings, we must stone a few women to death so that Mr. Saddam Hossein knows that the Islamic revolution has arrived.

In order to hold Friday Prayers in Basra, we must send a qualified, veteran Friday Prayers Leader who has experienced prison. The most highly qualified person for this task is His Reverence the Second Imam, Mr. Hossein-Ali Montazeri, who is now the Friday Prayers Leader of the holy city of Qom. We must assign his reverence to Basra as well, but since he does not have time on Fridays, Basra's Friday Prayers should be held on Thursdays or Saturdays to enable His Reverence Montazeri to be present.

Oh—I almost forgot. The honourable Students Following the Imam's Line, who have occupied the American Embassy, should decide on a quota of hostages for Basra right now, and they should allocate at least four hostages to the city once it is seized. Thus we will be able to fight international imperialism direct from Basra as well.

5 October 1980

Ayatollah Montazeri Clarifies

In His Lofty Name. Recently, some rumour-mongers have speculated that Ayatolah Montazeri has authorised that the American hostages in Tehran be circumcised. This is to announce that such an act would amount to interference in the United States' internal affairs. As we have no intention of interfering with any country's internal affairs, the rumours of circumcision are entirely fanciful.

Ayatollah Montazeri's Office,
Qom.

Notice to Beloved Demonstrators

Considering that according to laws inherited from the traitor Shah's era, all democratic demonstrations and marches should be held with prior notification so that the Government can also prepare themselves, beloved demonstrators are requested to provide the Provisional Revolutionary Government with the following details at least one day before beginning their march:

1. The route of the march
2. The slogans they will be shouting
3. The items with which they would like to be attacked:
   a.) Sticks b.) Stones c.) Firearms.

(NOTE: Should the beloved demonstrators not be able to choose one of the items themselves, the Provisional Revolutionary Government will be at liberty to select one, two or all three to suppress the demonstration.)

Finally, we would like to advise all those interested in opposition demonstrations to come on and make our day.

Revolutionary Prime Minister
Matey Mehdi Bazargan

24 August 1979

What Is Democracy?
An Essay by Sadeq Sedaqat

Our esteemed teacher last week gave us a very good subject for an essay, namely democracy, and this week, while that esteemed teacher is in prison, we explain democracy for the new teacher and our beloved fellow students.

What is democracy? It is obvious and self-evident that we do not know what democracy is. We also have a knowledgeable uncle who is very learned and has read as much as six shelf-loads of books, but even he doesn't know what democracy is. We therefore conclude that there are two types of democracy: the one that we do not know and the one that our uncle does not know.

One benefit of democracy is that there are many political parties in the society. We have an uncle who says the best of all parties is the ruling party, and he himself is always a member of the ruling party, but when we grow up we would like to join the Bend-with-the-Wind Party because we can afford its membership fees more easily.

In a democratic society, everything is decided by a majority vote and last year in the second term, when most of the students in our class were lazy, on the very day of

Religious Studies examination they wanted to blow up the heater in the classroom, and we were opposed to that but they acted democratically and voted beforehand and the lazy ones were in a majority and at the hour of the examination the heater was blown up and since we were near the heater we were burned too and the smoke filled our eyes but we were in a minority. We therefore conclude that in a democratic society those who are in the minority should stay away from the heater.

Last summer when we went to the village of Aliabad, we talked with our own aunty about democracy and our aunty is superstitious and knows many proverbs, and she told us that "democracy doesn't always pay." We therefore conclude that "the bird that will eat figs must have a crooked beak."

As we said earlier, in a democratic society no one can bully the people because it is the majority who decide everything and the people vote and elect one person and then that one person bullies them.

This was an essay on democracy by me, Sadeq Sedaqat, and we promise not to write any more such essays.

21 September 1979

The President's Diary—2

To the Army HQ in the morning. At the gate, a soldier salutes. I jump, thinking he wants to box me on the ear. But I pretend nothing has happened. It's not right for the Commander-in-Chief of the Forces to be scared by a soldier's salute. I return his salute very coolly, I mean I say "Hello" to him and go on. I enter General Fallahi's office. The officer there tells me to take a seat and says the General will be with me in half an hour. I sit down for some ten minutes, keeping myself busy with the Imam's *Explanation of Problems.* Then the officer asks me what my business is with the General. I tell him that it is a private matter. He asks if he can do anything to help. I say no, and ask him to contact the General wherever he is and tell him the President has arrived. Having heard that, the officer makes radio contact, and says: "Sir, someone from the President's office is here and wants to see you." It turns out General Fallahi is already in his office and this officer has been keeping me waiting because he doesn't know that I am the President. What's more, I don't understand this silly joke of theirs, speaking from one room to the next on the walky-talky.

Inside General Fallahi's office, I tell him what a dumb officer he's got who doesn't know me. He says he doesn't think he's even an officer, just someone that so-and-so clergyman, Beheshti, has sent along, insisting that he should work at General Fallahi's office. Now I understand why that officer didn't take us seriously. We spend some time discussing the war with General Fallahi. He has some strange things to say. For instance, he tells me that a rifle has a longer range than a pistol, a tank's range is even greater than that of a rifle, and that a Fantom can fly faster than ten tanks. We decide to go to the front at 4 p.m. But I later advise that we should go at 3 o'clock, because we shouldn't give these Iraqis any chance to overthrow the Islamic Republic in the interests of the world-predator America.

To the front in the evening. How much dust we eat! Right there I tell them to order the mayor of the front to pave these roads. We take cover in a bunker. The Iraqis fire a few missiles which land a few yards over there. All of a sudden, from inside the bunker next door, I hear the voice of Hossein Khomeini, the Imam's grandson, who shouts: "Fire!" Immediately two Revolutionary Guards rush a well-lit barbeque pit over to his bunker. Crawling on my stomach, I also get to the grandson's bunker. I see he is grilling kebabs. As Commander-in-Chief of the Forces, I move in, pick up a piece of bread and tell Master Hossein that the first lot should be mine. He selflessly offers me a skewer of grilled lamb kidney. Oh it's so tasty!

I'm supposed to spend the night at the front like the soldiers. A truck arrives, with the duvet, the mattress and pillows, but they've forgotten to send any sheets. I order them to purge the quartermaster. Then, as President and Commander-in-Chief of the Forces, I go to bed grumbling.

I don't know if it's four in the morning or noon when I wake up. I remember that I am to meet the Libyan Ambassador in Tehran. I head for Tehran with unwashed hands and face. On the plane I study the reports from various fronts, but I don't understand a word.

I spend some time talking to the Libyan Ambassador. The rascal speaks Arabic, so you can't understand what he says. At any rate, I guess it has to do with Libya's support for Iran, so I do not show any signs of disapproval. The Imam's son Master Ahmad comes over and complains that the Prime Minister Rajaie is a human being too and I shouldn't ignore him so completely, and that I could at least take him along when I go to the front. I say that, honest to God, I'm afraid that he might be hit by a bullet or a shell or something, and be hurt, and then the Islamic Republic would be left without a Prime Minister, and it's not easy to find someone like him, especially at a time when you cannot even find a navvy for construction work. Master Ahmad has a big laugh at what I say, I myself have a big laugh. We laugh with Master Ahmad for some five minutes.

Then the air-raid warning siren is broadcast on the radio, announcing a state of red alert. This means the Iraqi planes are going to attack in a few minutes and people should rush to their rooftops or the street to watch the bombers. Master Ahmad and I get up and go to the rooftop and for a while look around the sky like pigeon-trainers—gosh, those were the days. But nothing happens. Not even a pigeon flies.

We go downstairs and I ring up Hojatoleslam Mohtashami, head of the radio and television, and ask him why they've been blowing the warning siren these past few days for nothing. He says, "In the Name of Allah, the Compassionate, the Merciful, it's meant so the people don't think the war is over." I ask him what's wrong with the war being over and the people too thinking it was? He says, "In the Name of Allah, the Compassionate, the Merciful, because if the war is over we cannot go on ruling the people." I ask him if they're supposed to be ruling the country. He says, "In the Name of Allah, the Compassionate, the Merciful, yes!" I get angry and tell him, "Oh yeah, since when are you supposed to be in charge?" He doesn't answer me this time. He just says, "In the Name of Allah, the Compassionate, the Merciful," and hangs up. I for my part say, "There is no god but Allah," and bang the receiver down harder than any President has ever done.

I then hit the sack, since this is the only thing I can decide on my own.

25 October 1980

From the Supreme War Council

Dear compatriots!

At these sensitive and historical moments, it is observed that a group of rumour-mongers and counter-revolutionaries are spreading rumours to the effect that should the aggressor Iraqi forces withdraw from Iran, the Iran-Iraq war will come to an end.

It is necessary to remind the brothers and sisters that they should not pay any attention to these rumours, because the valiant, shroud-wearing Islamic Revolutionary Guards shall never let the Iraqi forces pull out of the areas they have occupied in Iran, and even should they leave Iran, the Islamic Republic will continue the war until Saddam Hossein is overthrown, the Palestine War has begun, Israel is bombed, Saudi Arabia is destroyed, King Hossein of Jordan has fallen, King Hassan of Morocco is punished, Soviet forces have left Afghanistan, Poland's internal problems are settled, the crisis in Bulgaria is over, and the British Labour Party's leadership problem is resolved.

Aided by God, assisted by the saints, and backed by the prayers of the Qom Friday Prayers Leader, we hope to overcome all these difficulties as soon as possible and then continue to fight the pagans with peace of mind.

(Fingerprints of Hashemi-Rafsanjani, Sheikh Mohammed Montazeri, Mostafa Chamran, and several other dubious characters.)

Communiqué

Recently it has been observed that some of the brothers and sisters in charge of revolutionary organs put their signatures at the bottom of their letters or on the circulars and communiqués that they issue. In view of the fact that "signing" is fundamentally an ungodly phenomenon and action in which the deposed Shah used to indulge, the Committee for the Prescription of Virtues and Prohibition of Vices wishes to remind the revolutionary sisters and brothers that they should refrain from signing any document as far as possible and, except where protocols of cooperation with foreign countries are concerned, they should resort to the Islamic method of fingerprinting.

It is evident that, in order to abide by religious tenets and observe the Islamic code, before pressing their fingerprints, the beloved sisters working at revolutionary institutions must wrap their fingers in a corner of their veils or scarves, or with a handkerchief or a piece of cloth, so that the direct imprint of their fingertips should not arouse the brothers.

And May Peace Be Upon You
(Fingerprint of the Islamic Guidance Minister)

The President's Diary—3

I still have no idea whether the hostages have been released. No one tells me what's going on. Back when they first occupied the American Embassy I used to be better informed, because of course, I was not President. I mean, they would come over and consult me on whom they should or should not take and what they should or should not do. And I would tell them whom they should take and what they should do. But nowadays I have to sit and wait for the radio to give me the news.

As I said, I was opposed to hostage-taking from the very first day. But by and by, as it was about to be decided that I should become President, I gradually changed my opinion in favour of it, but I still believe that hostage-taking should be done according to Islamic ideological guidelines, but those power-mongering, hegemonistic groups (whom I do not want to name now, nor even say what they look like nor which party they lead nor which mosque in Hamburg they used to run), they tried to establish that the President was a nobody and did not have the right to express opinions or to wield power.

Nowadays, because I go to the front every day, I do not

have time to deal with these people. They go to the Imam and tell him of me behind my back. The Imam listens and says nothing. I too go to the Imam and tell him of them behind their backs. The Imam frowns and says I should not interfere in such matters. So therefore, relying on the power of the people, who have decisively voted me their President, I tell these people nothing, so they can do whatever they want. Of course, I am not going to sit too quietly. I know how to deal with them, and I assure the Iranian people who have elected me, that they should rest assured that their elected President will stand up to these power-mongering, hegemonistic groups on the Day of Judgement and will take them to task. I assure you that most of them will go to Hell.

Now, after that introduction—which was necessary, because every now and then I must speak to the people frankly in the pages of my diary—there are some reports on matters accomplished which I should tell you about. Of course most of these things have not been done, but there is encouraging news from the front. This morning I heard that the Iraqis have captured our Oil Minister. I mean, they have desires on all our oil resources, even on our Oil Minister. I told this Mr Tondgouyan a thousand times to be careful. If I myself go to the front, well, I learned the tactics of warfare in the very early days of the war and the Iraqis cannot capture me. But the Oil Minister, who is not informed of military affairs, should not go to the front. Besides, this war of ours is such a mishmash that you don't know who's doing what. You ask about the Oil Minister, they tell you he's gone to the front. When you look for the

Army Commander, you find out that he's gone over to the Oil Company.

This afternoon there was news that one of the mullahs has overturned a tank near Birjand, in the east of the country. I told them there was no war in Birjand, and if this mullah really wanted to fight he should have gone to Khorramshahr. They told me he had panicked and had taken Khorassan Province for Khuzestan Province. I wonder why he overturned the tank, and if he had taken that for a donkey too.

I hear reports of the country's youth rushing to the front and embracing martyrdom in droves. I wish Mr Beheshti were among them.

Last night I slept at half past ten, but I had to get up at midnight, have a drink of water and then sleep again.

8 November 1980

Elections
An Essay By Sadeq Sedaqat

We beloved students know that elections are necessary for life and, just as a fish cannot live out of water, man cannot live without elections, and in elections ballot boxes are very useful to man, provided that man is a carpenter and has an order for the ballot boxes.

We have an uncle who is a carpenter and in his shop he has saws, planes, hammers and nails and makes ballot boxes for elections and used to make ballot boxes for elections before the Revolution too and yesterday when he came over to our house he told our father that the new ballot boxes were no different from the old ones.

On election day we got up early and went with our parents and our brother and sister to the countryside and played and had food there and came back at night and did not vote. Because our father says we must decide upon our lives for ourselves and go on a picnic, but if we vote, then others will determine our lives for us and we can't go on a picnic either.

This was an essay on elections by me, Sadeq Sedaqat, which I explained for the beloved teacher and students and we could not have explained it more clearly than this either.

12 April 1980

The President's Diary—4

In the Name of Allah, the Compassionate, the Merciful. Today it occurs to me that I might well be the busiest President in history, because from the time I wake up in the morning until I go to bed at night, I am busy writing articles and books. Writing this diary takes up a lot of my time. I also have to write newspaper editorials, which are printed under somebody else's byline. There're also the books I have ready for publication, and yesterday, on the way to the front, I went to a bookshop, met my publisher and we talked and haggled. They too have many problems and we spent a long time talking about the printing and binding of my books, so I couldn't make it to the front. We decided to leave the visit to the front for a more appropriate occasion.

We have a new book, my wife and I, on which we worked in Paris. Of course, she did the main work, but would not have her name on it, so it was published under my name. She used to argue that if someday, by chance, a woman were to become Iran's President and it happened to be her, these books might fall into the wrong hands, and people might use them to make fun of her. You know, the day

I told Jean-Paul Sartre that I was going to be Iran's first President, my wife was also there. Jean-Paul Sartre said: "So your wife is going to be Iran's first First Lady?" But my wife frowned and said: "No, I am going to be the first Madame President." The ideas these women get. Even I myself can't get on with the job, although I'm supposed to be a man.

I was saying: Right now most of my job is studies. Like a school kid who is behind with his homework, I have pen and paper in hand and keep writing all the time, at home, in the car, or at the front. The urge to become a writer is killing me. But despite all this I don't know why some people when they see me tell me that my writing has become boring, and that I am too verbose. And yet these same people take articles by that blah-blah Haj-Seyed-Javadi like hot cakes and xerox them, while *I* am their President.

They tell me that instead of so much verbiage I should act a little bit, that talking and writing all the time is not going to help sort things out. They tell me that in my writing I keep repeating myself and that I talk too much. Is this the way to behave towards an elected President? I tell them that maybe what they want is an illiterate President who would spell "soap" as "sope". They say even if he spells it as "sowp" and can use it to wash with, then it's soap, but if it doesn't clean, then it doesn't matter how it's spelled. Soap is something like henna, and it doesn't matter if you spell it with just one "n", like "hena". That is, if the henna won't dye, then it doesn't matter how it is spelled.

Well, that's one argument. Another argument is that you should see where the soap has come from, and for what reason it has been made. Well, where has the soap come from? From the soap factory. Now, how do you spell "soap factory"? If you spell it with an *e*, the "soap" too should be spelled with an *e* because it has come out of a "sope factory". If, however, you spell "sausage" with an *e*, then that would be wrong, unless it is a saus*e*ge which has come out of a *sope* factory. But since we know that sausages are made in sausage factories, then they are inevitably spelled with an *a*. This is a subject that I have studied in depth, and on which I have written a book, which I showed to Jean-Paul Sartre some fifteen years ago in Paris. (I'm not quite sure if it was Jean-Paul Sartre or Jean-Paul Belmondo, but I remember that I showed it to one of them and he liked it a lot.) But now, when I say the same things about soap and sausages, some people who mean to undermine the President say that I talk too much and that I write too much. One must find out who instigates these people and what is the root of this wave of opposition which in its causality, its quantitative shape and its qualitative form, is related to its philosophical subjectivity and objectivity. But some people say: "We don't understand what you write or what you want to say!" It may well be my fault, but then again, they might also be right!

9 May 1981

Hojatoleslam Dungollahi, a Man, a Legend

As the leading women's weekly in the land, The Fundamentalist Woman *finds itself duty bound to inform its readers of the innermost thoughts of the Nation's leading men. Every week, our combative sister Oriental "Orie" Fallacy, chief investigative reporter, seeks out and interviews an outstanding brother from the humble ranks of our Nation's leadership. In this edition, we proudly present Orie's in-depth interview with Hojatoleslam Dungollahi, a true son of the revolutionary village of Dungollahabad.*

Dungollahabad is a small village near the town of Khomein, the birth-place of our blessed, gracious Leader. In the past, it used to be called Dungeonollahabad because it is indeed built on the very same spot where, many decades ago, our beloved Imam's great-great-grandfather was jailed by a tyrannical local ruler who had unjustly accused him of having had an intimate relationship with one of his (the ruler's) mules.

When the mule gave birth to a calf with an uncanny resemblance to the Imam's great-great-grandfather, the local population celebrated the miracle by naming the jail where he had been held as Dungeonollah. Gradually, a settlement of pilgrims was formed around the mud-brick jail and, over the years, turned into the village we now know as Dungollahabad.

When the doors of the prisons were flung open at the Imam's command and the prisoners were freed from the shackles of the puppets of the world-predator America, Hojatoleslam Dungollahi was among the crowds who surged out of the jails, towards freedom.

He is now sitting in front of me, cross-legged, on an armchair, a man whose face bears the marks of many years of toil and suffering, and from whose chunky cheeks emanates a mysterious light that dazzles the eyes.

He insists that I should call him Dungo, as he was affectionately called for many years by the fellow-inmates in the Shah's chambers of horror. So, I begin my interview by asking brother Dungo how he felt on the day when the doors of the notorious torture houses were opened. His booming, well-modulated voice fills the room:

—Well, that day. Yes, on that day we suddenly heard a lot of noises and shouts and commotion and when we went to the door of the prison, we saw that it had been broken and the prisoners were rushing out.

Orie: Rushing out? Were you not in the prison yourself?

Dungo: No, not really. I was outside the door, with a box in my hand, for the people who had come over to visit their relatives.

Orie: Oh, a box! Full of leaflets?

Dungo: Leaflets?!

Orie: I mean, you were trying to give the visitors something secretly, so the police would not find out?

Dungo: Yes, that is right. We used to pass something to the visitors secretly.

Orie: And that's the way you used to fight the police?

Dungo: Fight? Yes, we would not let them find out what we were up to, because a few days before that they had nicked one of our mates.

Orie: What had he done?

Dungo: Well, just as I was doing, they had nicked him with a box of bootleg Winstons. But I was very careful. I wouldn't give American Winstons to just anybody.

I look into brother Dungollahi's piercing eyes. They are overflowing with a fighting spirit. It would seem that his eyes are engaged in a never-ending battle with my scarf and clothes. I put it to him that his struggle has changed the Nation's fate. I am overwhelmed by his modesty.

Dungo: Well, of course. I mean, I myself used to sell lottery tickets, because you couldn't get Winstons all the time, and there were many people whose fate would change with just one lottery ticket. In the same year when they sent the Imam into exile, one guy who had bought a ticket from me won fifty thousands toomans. He then came over and gave me ten toomans as a tip.

Yes, brother Dungollahi and thousands of other brothers like him, who in those days used to fight poverty and misery by selling bootleg American cigarettes and lottery tickets, are now well entrenched in the ranks of the militant clergy, waging a selfless, merciless war against international imperialism led by the world-predator America.

Hojatoleslam Dungollahi who, at the tender age of 35 is the Friday Prayers Leader of the mosque frequented by the capital's sizeable Dungollahabadi community, tells me about his prison days.

Dungo: Business was best on Mondays and Fridays, because the prisoners were allowed visitors on those days.

Orie: Have you never been in prison yourself?

It obviously takes brother Hojatoleslam Dungollahi an effort to overcome his reluctance to talk about his own imprisonment.

Dungo: The first time, I did three months, but someone had ratted on me.

Orie: Who?

Dungo: The boy himself.

With his head resting between the palms of his hands and in deep thought, Hojatoleslam Dungollahi has an uncanny resemblance to Plato, Socrates, or even Hojatoleslam Khalkhali. He goes on:

—You can't trust anyone, not even Mash Rajab the mule-handler's son.

Orie: Was he a SAVAK agent?

Dungo: A SAVAK agent?! How could he? He didn't have the guts for it. I was supposed to find him a job there myself, but they wouldn't have him. Then he told his parents everything! They took him to a doctor, and the cops put me in jail.

Orie: When did you join the ranks of the clergy?

Dungo: It was about three months before the Revolution. There were no lottery tickets and you couldn't find Winstons anywhere either. Business was pretty low. So I thought it was about time I started serving Islam.

Orie: And you put on the combat gear of the servants of Islam?

Dungo: I'd give my life for the Imam.

Orie: And the day the Imam came back, you were there at the airport to greet him?

Dungo: No, I wasn't. Because everybody had gone to the airport and the town was empty, me and a couple of other brothers were guarding the people's houses. Of course there were a few counter-revolutionaries who had gone to the airport, just to deceive the others and pretend they really loved the Imam. But by the time they came back home, we had impounded their property.

I look into Hojatoleslam Dungollahi's kind eyes. While I am taking notes, my scarf slips away, revealing some of the parts which must remain hidden to all men not admitted into the Muslim woman's privacy. As I make an effort to cover myself up, I hear Hojatoleslam Dungollahi's brotherly voice:

—Never mind, that's perfectly all right. It doesn't bother me.

Orie: Do you have a message for our readers?

Dungo: Tell them, on my behalf, that the only thing they

should look for is Islam. Today, it is Islam and the clergy who are in power. If it had not been for this Islamic Revolution, today our Nation would have been dragged into deviation and corruption with nothing to do but sell lottery tickets and bootleg American Winstons, and sodomise Mash Rajab the mule-handler's son. But today, thanks to our Glorious Islamic Revolution, even that boy has become the head of his neighbourhood Islamic Revolutionary Committee and nobody dares do to him what they did in the past.

We have a deadline to meet, but Hojatoleslam Dungollahi insists that I should stay on for supper. But the brother photographer says he must rush back to have the photographs printed, and dashes out of brother Dungollahi's house....

Mr Brick Interviewed

Q. Mr Brick, on the eve of the New Year, would you please
tell us about your role in the Iranian Nation's glorious
Revolution and also about what you did last year?

A. Well, you know, we're basically involved in construction and haven't got anything to do with politics. But
last year, because of the row between the Housing
Ministry and the Housing Foundation for the Deprived,
we were left completely idle. And if some of these
political groups had not come to our rescue and given
us something to do, then our role in the Revolution
wouldn't have been clear.

Q. Could you please tell us what they let you do?

A. Well, it was quite simple really, they'd throw us at people's heads. Last year a lot of my colleagues were
thrown into the University and, God willing, they're
going to get their degrees by the end of next year.

Q. What were your working arrangements?

A. They'd pick us up from construction sites. The days
when there'd be speeches at the University, they'd load
us into trucks and take us over in front of the campus.
There, there were people who'd throw us inside.

Q. Who were these people?

A. Honest to God, I don't know. They used to say they were members of the Party of Allah. They'd use a lot of us at opposition demonstrations, especially when there was going to be talk of freedom of speech.

Q. What is your personal view?

A. Well, I'm just a brick, I haven't got any particular views. As I said, our main job is construction. In those early days, there was talk of building houses for the poor. Then the people at the Housing Foundation for the Deprived started using us to build houses for themselves, and the Housing Ministry also got into the act, and when all the top people had their own houses, then nobody cared about us any more and we were lying about, doing nothing, until these politicos came along and picked us up and gave us a very decisive role in the Revolution.

16 March 1980

The President's Diary—5

In the name of Allah, the Compassionate, the Merciful.
Three books are keeping me busy right now, and I am
reading all three at the same time. After all, you can't
remain idle at the front. One was written by Napoleon,
another by our Shi'ite saint, the Imam Hossein's sister,
St. Zeynab, and the third is one of my own books, which
I'm reviewing so I won't forget what I've written.

When I read Napoleon, I appreciate the influence this
man could have had on certain people. When I read St.
Zeynab, I am really impressed by this esteemed lady's
manliness and her lofty ideas. When I read myself, I see
that I am better than either of them. That is to say, my
book includes both Napoleon and St. Zeynab. Just as I
myself do. In fact I am something between St. Zeynab and
Napoleon. I said this the day before yesterday in the jeep
to my Cultural Advisor, Moussavi-Garmaroudi, but he had
not gotten in the jeep yet.

I think that what they say that Napoleon has said, that
behind every successful man there is a kind woman, is right.
Of course I too help my wife at home. Cooperation at home
is an Islamic tradition. But because of some difficulties

which you know about, I cannot get round to doing the laundry as well, because the time I would waste washing a pair of underpants would amount to about 12 minutes, 30 seconds. Now in the same period of time, at the front, I could advance about 35.71 kilometers on foot, which, in the present circumstances, is quite necessary. That is to say, if we win this war, then all my theoies will prove right and this is good, both for the nation and for my publisher, and for Moussavi-Garmaroudi, whose briefcase was recently stolen and in it there was a lot of valuable material, and I, as the permanent, constant, irreplaceable and enfranchised representative of all the respectable citizens, ask the thief, or thieves, to keep the contents of the briefcase and deliver the case itself, which is of high quality leather, at the Presidential Palace to me or to Mr Moussavi-Garmaroudi, so that we can once again write valuable things and put them in it.

At this point, there is something to be said about the University, the closure of which cannot be justified, but one cannot readily consent to its being open either. So, it is best if its gates are left ajar. We will thus have reached both objectives, and our name shall be recorded in history's good books.*

* Universities were among the most prominent centres of opposition to Khomeini's regime. In the spring of 1981, the clerical faction of the regime organised a series of demonstrations led and aided by armed men, to close down Tehran University. Fearing that he might be outflanked by the mullahs, Dr Bani-Sadr led the march into Tehran University after a long siege that cost a number of lives. Once inside the campus, he addressed the club-wielding mob, saying, "Today we have established the Government's authority." This cost Dr Bani-Sadr dearly, especially as he had tried to attract the educated and professional groups to the cause of the Islamic Republic. (Translator's note)

There was a time when I ordered the club-wielders to storm the University, drive out deviant groups, and close it in order to establish the Government's authority, Now, on the other hand, I say that if the Government's authority is to be established with sticks and stones, that authority will be of no use to anyone except my aunty. Therefore, the secret of man's, as well as beast's, dynamism and evolution lies in these same differences in his beliefs, his views and his attitudes toward clubs, so that according to his interest, he will condone or condemn them. And this is a point which I discussed some fifteen years ago in a Paris café, with the present French President, Monsieur Mitterand, and he was so pleased that he paid for my coffee. So now that the socialist Monsieur Mitterrand has been elected President, he should concentrate solely on resolving the Palestinian problem, and in the message of congratulations that I cabled to him I emphasised this same point. I still haven't had a reply, but then again their teleprinter might have broken down.

At this point I am reminded of a story I read last night in *Mother Kolthoum's Tales*. How insightful is this old Mother Kolthoum in the domains of the quantitative and qualitative theories of infrastructural issues, in the breadth of philosophical history and the synthetic transmutation of unitarian conditions, and I have told Jean-Paul Sartre too about *Mother Kolthoum's Tales*, and I shall also tell you many of them, and tomorrow, on the front line under the barrage of enemy artillery and mortars, in the trenches where Islam is defended, I shall get down to writing some of them.

23 May 1981

Last Tango in Paris

In *Asghar Agha* some 40 days ago, we said that if Dr Bani-Sadr, recent resident of the Presidential Palace, also came to Paris, the probability of civil war in Iran would increase. And yet we did not know then that Dr Bani-Sadr would bring along a souvenir in the shape of a Prime Minister, namely Mr Masoud Rajavi, the Mojahedin leader. We can now safely assume that Bani-Sadr and Rajavi will also soon start fighting each other in order to be officially admitted into the ranks of the Paris-based opposition, known as "Popposition".

Political observers have described the arrival in France of Bani-Sadr and Rajavi as the "Last Tango in Paris" and speculate that within the next two weeks these two will launch their own newspapers in order to slander each other, and thus impress and encourage the Iranian Nation.

8 August 1981

Miracle

Following Mr Rajaie's landslide election as President, one of *Asghar Agha's* nosey correspondents asked the Interior Minister to explain how so may votes could have been cast while people never left their houses on election day. His Excellency the Minister replied: "It was a miracle."

1 August 1981

PART TWO

IN WHICH everyone waits
for the Imam to die...
(1981 to 1983)

The Death of an Imam

—Hello, Asghar Agha*? Is it true that Khomeini has died?*
—No, sir, it apparently isn't.
—I'm terribly sorry.
—The sorrow is ours!

For about a week now, we have been having such telephone conversations with our compatriots the world over. It all started when *Newsweek* interviewed President Khamenei and asked him if any decisions had been made as to who should succeed Khomeini. Khamenei replied, simply, that a three-man or a five-man council would be formed.

The World Service of the BBC carried a tantalizing version of this story before *Newssweek* appeared on the newsstands. In the meantime, the ailing Khomeini cancelled his meetings, as usual, for two weeks in order to rest. Then rumours spread that Khomeini had died. Some reports claimed he hadn't died, but had been taken to a hospital in Zurich. Others said, "No, they've taken his body to Switzerland."

Last Wednesday the Islamic Republic issued a statement denying " the Iranian exiles' slanders" about Khomeini's death and saying that he would soon re-appear in public to put an end to all such rumours.

Now, Khomeini may well have really died. He might even have died on the very day that the Shah's regime collapsed, thus forcing the Islamic Republic officials to stage a cover-up. But at any rate, considering the present situation and the state of the nation, just as an elephant would be worth 100 toomans whether dead or alive, Mr Khomeini too would be worth 95 toomans, dead or alive! (That's a special five-tooman discount for the opposition.)

The latest reports say the three-man council that will succeed Khomeini has been formed and includes Grand Ayatollahs Montazeri, Golpayegani and Mar'ashi.

Ayatollah Montazeri has announced that the three-man committee will be chaired by Imam Khomeini!

5 February 1982

What Will You Do If the Imam Dies? An Essay by Sadeq Sedaqat

In the name of Allah, the Compassionate, the Merciful. It is of course obvious and self-evident that should the Imam, may peace be upon him, die, I, Sadeq Sedaqat, will clean and dust my house and will destroy any sweets, nuts, candies or chocolates that there may be in the house because after the explosion at the Islamic Republic Party's nest of spies and the martyrdom of Ayatollah Beheshti, the Revolutionary Guards would arrest and interrogate anyone who was walking along the streets with a box of sweets in his hands, or with a smile on his lips, in order to find out why they had bought sweets or why they were smiling. I, Sadeq Sedaqat, in addition to purging my house of sweets and nuts, even biscuits and lollipops, would also put a grim look on my face and would even cry while walking along the streets.

I, Sadeq Sedaqat, because I have not been a fundamentalist, or a revolutionary, so far while walking along the streets, I did not know the proper way of walking, so therefore, the day the Shah died abroad, and I did not know about it, while walking along the streets tears flowed from my eyes, because there was a nail in my shoe which was hurting my foot, and my eyes had taken pity on my foot, and because my foot could not itself cry, my eyes were crying on its behalf. As the poet has said:

On any limb should life inflict some pain,

Instead of it the eyes will cry like rain.

And as I was crossing the road with tears in my eyes, two Revolutionary Guards aimed their guns at me and ordered me to stop, and another Revolutionary Guard held me from behind with both his hands and ordered me to stop and I asked him what sort of a halt order that was because when you put your arms around someone from behind, why do you then order them to stop as well? Those Revolutionary Guards thought I had hidden the Shah's picture at the bottom of my shoe and was crying. They beat me up and took my shoes off and my foot felt good and my tears stopped and I started laughing.

Those guardians of Islam thought I, Sadeq Sedaqat, was mad, so they apologised to me, and went away and told me they had thought I was crying over the Shah's death. Because on that day, they were arresting anyone who was crying on the streets.

I, Sadeq Sedaqat, on that day took the advice of the Revolutionary Guards and hung it from my ears like an earring, and I flattened the tip of that nail with a pestle, and from that day on, when crossing the roads, I would always smile and snap my fingers.

But one day, as I was snapping my fingers while walking along the streets, once again some Revolutionary Guards held on to me from the front and the back and ordered me to halt! "What's the matter?" I asked. They told me that I was smiling and snapping my fingers because Ayatollah Beheshti had been blown up the night before. I said I had not known about that, and told them that I had always smiled and snapped my fingers. But they did not believe me. I took those Revolutionary Guards to some of the local shops and asked the shopkeepers whether it was not true that I always snapped my fingers while passing through that area. They said that it was. So therefore the Revolutionary Guards believed that I was innocent and told me they had thought I was happy because Ayatollah Beheshti had been killed, because on that day they were arresting anyone who was happy or who had bought sweets.

So therefore, if the Imam, may peace be upon him, dies, I, Sadeq Sedaqat, will be sad and unhappy and will put a few big nails through the sole of my shoe, and will walk along the streets with tears in my eyes, so that the Revolutionary Guards will have nothing to do with me.

This was myself, Sadeq Sedaqat's essay on the Imam's death, which I shall finish right now because there is a lump in my throat and the nails in my shoe are sticking into my foot, and the rest of which I shall write, God willing, after the Imam dies.

Amen, O Lord of Both Worlds.

On the Hazards of Smoking
An Essay by Sadeq Sedaqat

In the Name of Allah, the Compassionate, the Merciful. I, Sadeq Sedaqat, will now expound to the beloved students on the subject of "Explain the Hazards of Smoking", because smoking is a most hazardous thing and causes the diseases of cancer and queuing. My very own uncle, who has been suffering from cancer for several years, travels abroad every year with the permission of the Government's Medical Commission, enjoys himself and smokes lots of cigarettes at low prices and then returns to the beloved homeland. Nonetheless, our father, who suffers from queuing, has developed blisters on the soles of his feet, and every day, first thing in the morning, goes to the cigarette queue and announces his presence, to do his bit, and returns home at four in the afternoon, having been beaten up, and borrows two cigarettes from our uncle. As the poet says: "Early to bed, early to rise, is still no reason you'll make it smokewise."

Myself, Sadeq Sedaqat, also did some research in order to write this essay, and we asked our local Friday Prayers Leader about the hazards of cigarettes, but that Prayers

Leader said to myself, Sadeq Sedaqat: "My dear boy, there's no way you could lose anything on account of cigarettes!" I said: "But there is." But His Grace said: "No matter how you account for it, there is no way you could lose. Even if you account for it rationwise, again it doesn't make any difference and you can't lose."

That Prayers Leader then said to myself: "I'm glad that you too have started thinking of getting involved in business—most of the kids in your neighbourhood work for me!" He then produced a carton of cigarettes from under his cloak and gave it to myself and said: "Sell this for 1,500 toomans on the black market and take two hundred toomans as your own share!"

The Prayers Leader then kindly took the address and the identity card of myself, Sadeq Sedaqat, from me and also said if I didn't pay him for the cigarettes by evening, first thing the next morning I would be sent to the front in order to combat the Ba'athist mercenaries.

Having sold those cigarettes to our own dear father, and having charged him 2,000 toomans and having said that we couldn't possibly take anything less, because if we did they'd send us to the front, we took our own share of 700 toomans and gave 1,300 toomans to the local Prayers Leader, and he, as an encouragement, gave us a bar of opium to sell for 4,000 toomans. As the poet has wisely said:

Seek knowledge and learn to be great,

And then they'll all want to be your mate.

Another hazard of smoking is giving signals to the enemy, because in the first days of the War of Right Against Falsehood, when there were blackouts every night, our own father, who was running across the yard towards the out-house with a roll of toilet paper in his hand, had a burning cigarette in his other hand, and in the darkness of the night, the Iraqi reconnaissance planes and bombers which were equipped with binoculars and telescopes and microscopes and were several thousand feet up in the sky, did not see the light of my dear father's cigarette, but our neighbour who is a member of the Thirty-Six-Million-Strong Intelligence Organisation, did see it and informed the Revolutionary Guards, and the brother Revolutionary Guards attacked from over the roof of our house, and myself, thinking they were Ba'athist mercenaries, started fighting them back, and shouting loud "I shall kill, I shall kill, the murderer of my brother, I will!" loud enough to put a shudder down our own spine. Our father had also barricaded himself in the outhouse and was issuing orders like a military commander, telling myself to go and call the brother Revolutionary Guards! At this moment one of the brother Revolutionary Guards went to the door of the toilet and shouted: "Come on out! The brother Revolutionary Guards know about it already!"

And thus, the father of myself, Sadeq Sedaqat, was charged with collaborating with Iraq, helping the Ba'athist forces in their bombardment of Tehran, and having links with international zionism, and was guided to solitary confinement in Evin prison and after he had been proven innocent was fined five million toomans.

Altogether, cigarettes have many hazards and countless benefits which depend on the way they are used during war or peace. Altogether, this was myself, Sadeq Sedaqat's essay on the hazards of cigarettes which was penned by myself.

Friday Prayers Sermon—1

"In the Name of Allah, the Compassionate, the Merciful.
The esteemed ladies and gentlemen who have come from
afar and are heedful to the news, to rumours and such
stories and are heedful to America, where the President
of the United States has been hit by a rifle, or maybe a
pistol, but he hasn't died. But of course this Reagan will
die in the end, like most Americans, like all of America.
Like all the people of the world who will finally be chopped,
all of them. How many crimes this Reagan has committed!
What an offering he made to Islam with that assassination,
that youth who guided the pistol. But his hand trembled.
But if his hand had not trembled, he would have fired his
shot so mightily that it would have hit this Reagan in the
middle of the head and would have blown it to fifteen pieces
that skull of his. All the pieces would have gone to Hell
separately. A president who is sinful, a president who is
arrogant, a president who does not walk the straight path,
our fundamentalist fighters will not tolerate such a president
of evil. They cut him off with a pistol. It is begot of the
Muslims that bullet in the magazine. They are begot of
the Muslims, that trigger and that breechblock which are

not in the magazine. We have three types of president in Islam. We can have a dead or executed president, that is one type. We can have a live president, that makes two types. And we can have a president-in-limbo, who is neither dead nor alive, and that makes three types, and this one our youth cannot suffer and so they sacrifice him with a pistol.

"It is because of all these sacrifices that we are in a good mood. When there is no blood-letting everybody gets bored, even some who are already bored. They must shed blood these youth as an offering, for the sake of bloodshed they must shed blood. For the sake of all they must shed. It has blessings for us, blood does, for everybody. What they say, these liberals and nationalists, is that blood has got plasma, has got red cells and has got white cells, blood has. They are heretics, they have got it all wrong, blood has got only blessing. And even if it has white cells or it has red cells, it is fighting for Islam, that white cell is, and it is fighting for Islam, that red cell too. That green cell is fighting for Islam. All the corpuscles, whatever colour they be, they are for Islam. They must convert to Islam, the corpuscles must. They must become Muslims, the mercenary Iraqi corpuscles. It must convert to Islam, that plasma. There should be black cells in our blood instead of white ones. Instead of red ones. Instead of pistachio ones. They should not conspiratorise. All are equal in Islam. All are of the same colour, all corpuscles are, in Islam. Everywhere, in the basement too they are of the same colour, just as on the rooftop. You should call 'Allah is the Greatest' on the rooftops, on ladders. You must not dodge your duty. That youth who gunned Mr Reagan, he dodged not his duty in America. I warn the doctors in Mr Reagan's hospital. I give them my final ultimatum that they should treat him not. They should stitch up no part of him which has been hit with the pistol. That would be stitching up the infidel. That is not permitted in the Quran, that someone should stitch up a lewd man, or connect a drip to his arm. We have given so many martyrs. We have given too few. It is not sufficient. There was a plot against families under the heathen Shah which was enforced with pills and instruments, but we control the population without any devices so that it is reduced, the population is. So they are planned, the families are. Whether boys, or girls or whatever. It is not the case that we do not plan or control the population. Even the intellectuals. What are they saying, those writers? They are not writers, they're not. They are not writers, those writers. They are not people's writers. They are not the *People*, they are not. They are not the masses' newspaper. The communist Tudeh Party who make the *Mardom* newspaper, they are doing a good job. What is good is good. What is evil is evil. The film *Cow* which I said was a good film, that film was good. That cow was good. This Mr Kianouri, their leader, is also good. This Tudeh Party is also good, whose First Secretary is the grandson of our great-uncle, Sheikh Fazlollah Nouri, executed 80 years back for standing up against the satanic Constitutional Revolution, who was a true revolutionary, that Sheikh Fazlollah Nouri was. He was martyred. But the radio and television too must be corrected. It should not be the case that a television breaks down and shows snow flakes or that a radio has a burned-out tube. Do not conspiratorise. Do not stitch. They should not stitch up Mr Reagan, those doctors should not, because in Kurdestan too they are executed, the doctors who stitch up the stitch-less guerrillas. Who stitch up Satan's stitch-less Fadaiyan. But do not be stitchers-up. May peace be upon you, and Allah's graces, and so on and so forth.''

18 April 1981

Financial News

It is reported that, in an effort to free themselves from financial difficulties, the Islamic Republic's economists are selling the country's gold reserves and have so far sold some forty tons of gold at below-market prices.

Commenting on the report, His Eminence Ayatollah Montazeri, the Islamic Republic's only Esteemed Juriconsult, told our economics correspondent, "These gold reserves are second-hand, they're leftovers from the previous regime. So we sold them at half price."

Asked whether the sale of the country's gold reserves would not lead to currency devaluation and inflation, the Esteemed Juriconsult said: "The picture of Qom's Feizieh Seminary is printed on our new bank notes. They don't need any other backing."

Confirming the Esteemed Juriconsult's comments, the Governor of the Central Bank said: "What His Eminence Ayatollah Montazeri has in mind is the spiritual backing for the bank notes. Their material backing is the large numbers of 'In His Lofty Name' and 'Allah is the Greatest' that we have available in the Treasury."

* * *

On the anniversary of the Revolution, the Islamic Republic has issued its new 100-tooman bank notes, which carry pictures of Qom's Feizieh Seminary on one side and Jerusalem's al-Aqsa mosque on the other.

According to our correspondent, due to the attractive pictures printed on them, the new 100-tooman notes are bought and sold in the market for as much as seventy or even eighty toomans each.

20 February 1982

Profession

It so passed that I chanced upon this mullah with a questionnaire in his hand. He gave it to me to fill in for him, excusing himself that he did not have his glasses with him. Or perhaps it was that he did not have his mastery of words with him.

I seized a plume and asked his name. "Hassan, Pilgrim of Blessed Mecca, Exalted Kerbela and Holy Meshed," said he. "Surname?" asked I. "Ever praying," replied he. "Religion?" I enquired. "Muslim," he answered. "Profession?" I queried. He shuffled about and then whispered in my ear: "Write 'Muslim' against that too."

Describe the Spring
An Essay by Sadeq Sedaqat

It is obvious and self-evident that we beloved students must describe the spring every year, because the spring is a describable season and great scientists have described the spring every year and last year when we were in the second class we described the spring, and the year before that when we were not coming to school we used to describe the spring for ourselves at home, and this year when our dear teacher was purged and they brought us another teacher instead we have written on the subject of "Describe the Spring" like every year. Now the description of the spring by myself, Sadeq Sedaqat, of Class 3-C.

Spring is a beautiful and pretty and charming and refreshing season which altogether is an ungodly season, because flowers are ungodly and blossoms are also ungodly and in this season the bosom of nature is filled with flowers and the rest of her body is also filled with flowers and one is intoxicated by scent of the flowers and one is then lashed at the *Komiteh*.

Spring also comes in various types and forms. One type of spring is "the Spring of Freedom", which is the season when they close down newspapers and shut down magazines and strangle journalists. In this season truncheons grow by the sides of brooks and bearded nightingales sit on branches and in this season trees are rejuvenated and they tie the Kurds to the trees and shoot them.

Last spring, we and our family and our father and mother and sister and brother went to Ali-abad and went to our aunt's place, but our aunt was not in and they had taken her to the *Komiteh* and they had said that she had been in contact with the SAVAK but our aunt had given her golden bracelets and necklace to the head of the *Komiteh* and it had been found out that she had not been in contact with the SAVAK and she came back home and kissed us and gave me a present for the new year and said, "My dear Sadeq, God willing, when you grow up you'll become a lout and a mugger and you'll become the chief of the *Komiteh* here and you'll give me back my jewellery."

Another use of spring is that it is the season of prosperity and abundance and in this season the sheep become pregnant and in Australia and Argentina and America they give birth and multiply and are exported to our country and help our economic programs. We therefore conclude that sheep too know something about economics.

Altogether, spring is a likeable season because in this season one falls in love with the neighbour's daughter and every day looks through the window to see her sitting on the balcony, reading, but then along comes the Foundation for the Deprived* and kicks them out and expropriates their house and we no longer see the neighbour's daughter and every day see the head of the Foundation for the Deprived who is sitting on the balcony reading the *Towzih-ol-Massael.** Therefore we conclude that charity begins at home.

And that was the essay "Describe the Spring" which I, Sadeq Sedaqat, wrote and I have also written a poem about spring which I shall explain below:

Comes the spring and nature is rejuvenated,

O Sadeq Sedaqat, you must become educated.

For the second spring of freedom, you must not so much fret,

O Sadeq Sedaqat, you ain't seen nothin' yet.

* "Foundation for the Deprived" is a post-revolutionary organisation which controls a vast economic empire inside and outside Iran, made up of expropriated agricultural land, industries and urban property.

* *Towzih-ol-Massael* or "explanation of problems" is the general title of the books on Shi'ite Islam's rules and regulations governing the believers' everyday lives. They have become notorious for their explicit discussion of sexual matters.

Friday Prayers Sermon—2

"But however, in the Name of Allah, the Compassionate, the Merciful. To the ladies and gentlemen who have come from the atomic reactor centre in order to heed our words, we have spoken time and again about the atom, but however, atomic reactors have been vital to Islam. In agriculture there are two things that have always weighed deeply. The second one is the tractor; the first one, however, is the reactor. The reactor, which is made of atoms, this reactor is, but however, the atoms of this are somewhat bigger than the atoms of the tractor, which they measure very carefully in these centres, they measure all of them carefully in spans, lest, Heaven forbid, one atom should be an inch or two bigger than another; one or the other of the two atoms, they should be measured. [The congregation say in unison: 'May Allah send Benediction and Peace upon Mohammad and His Descendants.'] But however, there are different issues about this subject of atoms and reactors and so on. So that it should be made known about the atomic reactors of which there have been some found in secret hideouts, everybody should be watchful of his neighbour, atomic reactorwise. Everybody should be careful of his neighbour's house, so that if in case, Heaven forbid, should someone have hidden a reactor in this or that corner, this should be made manifest*. Or that mother who came here and said unto us that her son was making an atomic reactor in her basement, these, these mothers who are there to bear witness, to bear witness if anybody is conspiratorising against Islam and the Muslims, Heaven forbid, with a reactor or a tractor or what, or that there was a mother, and Italian one, written up in the *Guardian* newspaper in English last week on Monday, who this mother set fire to herself on account that she was worried by the news that they slaughter the innocents in the Islamic Republic. But however, what has it got to do with Italy? We will bear none of this. If, Heaven forbid, the mother of our own Master Ahmad should now come here and want to set herself on fire, to make a fireworks display of herself, to light herself like a bonfire for others to jump over, we shall not stop her, that mother, but however, we shall pour kerosene and gasoline over her in accordance with the prescription of virtues. Someone who wants to protest against the killing of these children who are here, like that mother who set fire to herself, she will go to Hell, that mother will. She will be burned once again in Hell. She will be burned twice. What did you think? There is no

---

*1. Following Khomeini's call for mutual spying throughout society, there were reports in Iran's state-controlled press of parents turning in their children who were allegedly involved in anti-regime activities. At least one such young man was executed after allegedly being informed on by his mother. Iranian television broadcast an interview between the repentant son and his mother before his execution.

foolery here. Mr Pope, too, if he too wants to set himself on fire, we will do some more burning. It is not the case that we will not kill any more. But however, we have made a revolution for the atomic reactor. It was the staff of the atomic reactor centre who made the revolution with bare hands. With a bare reactor. How important it has been this atom in Islam! They ought to be careful about the making of the reactor. It should not be the case that one day, Heaven forbid, we shall be needful of the foreigners' atomic reactor. It must be Islamic, the atomic reactor must. The Prophet of Islam himself, when he had nothing to do at home, he would make reactors three times as big as this one. Maybe even more. But however, I pray for all of you, for all reactors, for all atoms, may you all be fruitful, and may there be ripeness in your work, in everybody's work, in the reactor's work. May peace be upon you, and this and that.''

5 December 1981

Explain the Benefits of Agriculture
An Essay By Sadeq Sedaqat

In the Name of Allah, the Compassionate, the Merciful. Of course we dear students know that agriculture is necessary for living things and their fathers and their mothers because in agriculture one plants wheat and apples and trees and it is also useful for cleaning the air and they also eat its fruits. As the poet says:

A fruit tree you must plant,

Or of fruits you'll be scant.

One of the fruit trees is the apple tree and it is planted in various agricultural areas and we know one apple tree which is very famous and it is in a village in France and anyone who sits under it will become forgetful and will interfere in politics and his son-in-law too will interfere in politics and even his grandson will interfere and anyone who sits under that tree will become a king. And as the poet has wisely said:

No pain, no gain,

He who sits under the apple tree will reign.

Myself, Sadeq Sedaqat, was born to an agricultural family and our father was in agriculture, and before the

Revolution he used to sell lottery tickets in front of the Ministry of Agriculture. But after the Revolution attention was paid to agriculture and that father does not sell lottery tickets anymore and sells bootleg whiskey and attends the Friday Prayers too and during the prayers says to the man next to him: "Allah is the Greatest. May Allah save us from the demons. Johnny Walker 500 toomans." And the man next to him, if he is into that kind of thing, will understand that these words are not Arabic and will say: "May Allah guide us along the straight and narrow. Can you get us some cognac tomorrow?" And our father says: "There is no deity but Allah. No cognac, I'm just a whiskey-wallah." Then they both salute the Prophet and having said their prayers they go away together. We therefore conclude that Friday Prayers promote unity.

Another benefit of agriculture is the planting of tulips, the planting of which is easier than other flowers and the best way to do that is to be martyred so that tulips will grow from our blood and we had seven brothers, three of whom were martyred under the previous regime and three of whom were martyred under the new regime but no tulips grew from the grave of any of them because being martyred under torture does not count and no tulips will grow, but as for our other brother, they came along from the Revolutionary Committee and they beat him up to volunteer him to go to the front and, Allah willing, this one will grow tulips.

In the old days when agriculture was not booming, we used to import wheat and rice and vegetables and fruit from foreign countries but fortunately after the Revolution we no longer import from abroad because we are under an economic blockade.

Another type of agriculture is sowing the seeds of discord and we have a brother who is in the Tudeh Party and he sows the seeds of discord and reaps them with a sickle and whenever we object he smashes our head with a hammer. As the poet has wisely said:

> In one hand a sickle, the Imam's picture in the other,
> That's the only way I wish to dance, brother.

This was my own, Sadeq Sedaqat's, essay, which was recited for the esteemed seminarians in Class 3-C.

Amen, O Lord of Both Worlds.

Crime Report

According to Islamic Republic radio, the Kuwaiti Government has detained five members of the Muslim Iranian Nation on charges of listening to the Voice of the Islamic Republic and has repatriated them.

This is not the first time that a foreign government has arrested VIR's listeners. The regime occupying West Germany also recently jailed a group of devout members of Allah's Party. The West German government claims that the detainees had attacked the Iranian students' dormitory and had beaten up and badly injured 28 students. The truth of the matter, however, is that they had done nothing but listen to the Voice of the Islamic Republic.

And in Britain, only a few months ago, three beloved brothers were in their car listening to the Voice of the Islamic Republic when their automobile blew up. The police deviously claimed that they had been carrying a bomb!

Meanwhile, Ayatollah Montazeri, the only Esteemed Juriconsult in the Islamic Republic, has ordered the head of the Islamic Republic's Radio and Television to have the Voice of the Islamic Republic lower its transmission volume, so that the good brothers abroad can listen to it secretly, without fear of detection.

Reliable Radio

According to the Tehran dailies *Kayhan* and *Ettela'at*, an Iraqi university student who has been expelled from his country has said, "Most Iraqis believe Iranian radio." Asked by *Asghar Agha's* correspondent to explain why this was so, the Iraqi student said, "It's because they don't know Persian."

Struggle

"You know, I don't believe you can do anything from abroad."

"Another coffee?"

"No sugar, please. Whatever you want to do, it has to be done inside the country. Thanks."

"But I was there only two weeks ago. The coffee's getting cold. And the people there say it's the opposition outside the country who should do something. You see, there, they can't do anything, they can't even speak up, because of the repression and the guns and all that. We who're abroad must do something so the world hears their cry. I mean, really, in the future, aren't we going to feel ashamed of ourselves because we've been sitting here all the time, doing nothing, saying everything should be sorted out back there. Can I have the teaspoon, please?"

"You see, my dear, it's the people *inside* the country who ought to make up their minds and do something. Here, we're not really in touch with what's going on there. First, they should make some noise, or start a riot or a rebellion or something, and then we can follow that spark."

"No, my dear—have some cake too—that spark, you see,

must come from abroad, and then the people inside the country should follow it.''

"You know what?''

"What?''

"I say the only leader who can save the country is someone who is both inside *and* outside the country at the same time.''

"But that's not possible!''

"Of course it is! You just need a real man, with enough guts to go to the border area, put one foot across the border, inside the country, and the other foot over on this side of the border, outside the country, and then yell out that he's come to rescue the country.''

"What will happen then?''

"Well, it's obvious, really, because what will happen is that the people will go to him both from outside *and* from inside the country because they'll all feel he's one of them.''

"Well, I think you've got it all wrong; something totally different might happen.''

"Like what?''

"Well, as this guy is putting one of his legs across the border, on the other side, and the other leg this side, the barbed wire fence along the border will tear up his guts, not to mention his manhood.''

"Just like that?''

"Yes, just like that.''

"What do *you* think we should do then?''

"I think, you know, that this nonsense, this 'they've got to do it, and we've got to follow' and all that—I think none of this is going to get us anywhere.''

"What should we do then?"

"We should not wait for each other. Each one of us must do his own bit, so that while we're rescuing the country as quickly as possible, we also make sure that our future leaders don't lose their manhood."

"I'm all for that. Could you pass the fork, please?"

"Sure, and let's just finish this cake before we rescue the country."

Bulletin

There are reports that upon hearing the news that the war has come to an end, Imam Khomeini has had a heart attack and has been hospitalised at the Heart Hospital's Queen Mother Suite. The Imam's doctors have prescribed that fighting should be resumed along the country's western borders within 24 hours.

29 May 1982

Knowledge or Wealth, Which is Better? An Essay by Sadeq Sedaqat

It is of course obvious and self-evident to us dear students, that neither knowledge is better nor wealth. Because we had an uncle who was very knowledgeable and used to read books all the time, and the other week they came over from the *Komiteh* and took his books away and took him to the *Komiteh* and beat him up so badly that he fainted. But we have another uncle who is very rich, and the day before yesterday they took *him* to the *Komiteh* and took his money from him and they also beat him up and he too fainted. We therefore conclude that the *Komiteh* is better.

In our neighbourhood there is a *Komiteh* and whenever we pass by that *Komiteh* we say ''hello'' to the Pasdars (Revolutionary Guards) but they do not answer back. A Pasdar is a creature who has a gun and he also has whiskey and he hangs his gun on his shoulder but not the whiskey. And we have an uncle who buys whiskey from that Pasdar and pays him 800 toomans and that Pasdar gives him a sack of rice and our uncle brings the rice home and opens the sack and pushes the rice aside and takes the bottle of whiskey out of the sack.

We must love the Pasdars and respect them because in Kurdestan they kill our Kurdish brothers and in the cities they lash anyone who plays backgammon because backgammon is against Islam and the Prophet and the blessed imams never played backgammon and one day when our father was playing backgammon with our uncle the Pasdars came in and there were also two tanks at the door and a truckload of Pasdars waiting round the corner and three Pasdars came in with their machine-guns and told our father and uncle to raise their hands and our father raised his hands and our uncle dropped the dice and then he too raised his hands and one of the Pasdars shouted, "Dice up!" And our uncle picked up the dice and raised them too. Then those Pasdars made our father and our uncle lie down on the floor and they wanted to lash them one hundred times each but then they pitied them and said they would accept 500 toomans for each lash and our uncle paid up 50,000 toomans and was not lashed but our father did not have any money and read them some classical poems by Hafiz and Sa'di and gave them lectures on history and geography and biology and physics and chemistry because he is a high school teacher, but the Pasdars said that was no good and they gave him one hundred lashes. We therefore conclude that here wealth is better than knowledge because if one has money one can save one's bottom but if one is knowledgeable and knows poetry and has memorised physics and chemistry and biology and history and geography that will be no good for one's bottom and one's bottom will receive the one hundred lashes. Therefore we students conclude that having wealth helps one raise one's bottom with pride.

But knowledge too has many benefits, because if one is knowledgeable and has some knowledge of theology and is a leading theologian people will accept whatever one says and even if one lies people will believe one's lies and if one does injustice people will put up with it and will applaud one and sacrifice sheep for one.

This was the essay written by me, Sadeq Sedaqat, which I wrote at the *Komiteh* because they have arrested us and brought us here because we were selling the opposition newspaper *Mojahed* and if we express regret for what we have done and promise not to sell that newspaper again they will not execute us and will only give us a life sentence because we have not done anything.

Amen, O Lord of Both Worlds

29 May 1982

The Imam's Will

Since the day the Imam, may peace be upon him, wrote his will and delivered it to the Majlis, the arisen, stricken and slain Nation has overflowed with joy and enthusiasm, and hearts have been filled with the hope that the Imam, may peace be upon him, has finally decided to die.

Wrapped in Iran's tricolour (now bearing the insignia of a crab, rather than the former lion and sun), the Imam's will was taken by Master Ahmad Khomeini to the Majlis [Parliament] last week. One copy of the will has also been handed to the Assembly of Experts, who are to open it after the death of the Imam, may peace be upon him, and benefit from His Grace's Imam-like, wise utterances.

Now that we have informed you that the Imam's will has been delivered, allow us to present you with a full copy of its text. Although this text was to have been revealed after the Imam's death, we have decided to speed things up by quoting the draft pages which our special correspondent has recovered from the Imam's rubbish bin.

"In the Name of Allah, the Compassionate, the Merciful.

"We are so warmed that this Will is going to be opened by you! But however, what a pity. We are, God bless Our

Soul, sad to have become dead at the youthful age of eighty-five. But however, we must all die. Mr Pope will die too. So will also Mr Saddam. It has not been the case that one person should have become dead, while another should have stayed alive.

"But however, with respect to what We have said with regard to the Will, that such should be carried out after We will have become dead, these are as follows:

"Article 2. With respect to why this Will has not had a first article, We are sorrowed that unfortunately We have been forgetful about that.

"Article 4: All must be heedful.

"Article 5: They must behave themselves.

"Article 6: Let them not conspiratorise.

"Article 7: They must not do something which.

"Article 8: Will make us become angry.

"Article 9: But however.

"Article 10: Article 9 *is* "But however"! Nothing funny about that.

"Article 11: They must not chew gum in government departments.

"Article 12: Nowhere.

"Article 13: Proximate that microphone here.

"Article 14: What does he have to say, this Mr Pope?

"Article 15: I would have stricken this Mr Pope in the mouth, if I had been alive.

"Article 16: But misfortunately (Note 1. That is to say unfortunately.)

"Article 17: Everybody must struggle against imperialism. The Islamic Nation must trample on the

American flag. (Note 2: Should they have spread one of that flag on this Blessed Soul's grave, the people will trample it automatically for the happiness of this Blessed Soul.)

"Article 18: But however, they should not get an undertaker to wash this Blessed Soul's body. They should get instead someone from a public bath to wash this Imam like living ones.

"Article 19: Ahmad should not be so tearful.

"Article 20: Have three oppositionists executed by Our grave on the third night after Our death.

"Article 21: Have seven Bahai's executed by Our grave on the seventh night after Our death.

"Article 22: Have forty Tudehis amnestied by Our grave on the fortieth night after Our death, should they have been repentful of conspiratorising.

"Article 23: Nothing.

"Article 24: But however, that article was meant for those reporters who will be curious about how We may have felt about Iran.

"Article 24: Again nothing.

"Article 25: The animal with which you will have obtained copulation, its meat you must not be allowed to eat, out of respect, which We had already said in Our *Towzih-ol-Massael* while We were still alive.

"Article 26: They must have Our grave made two feet less deep so as We will be closer to God.

"Article 27: Our body should take a bullet-proof car. (Note: Its coffin should also be proofed against bullets.)

"Article 28: They should take Our coffin on foot from

Our house to Freedom Square, but there should be nobody inside it. (Note: The crowd must not trample on Mr Bazargan.)

"Article 29: That's quite a lot of articles so far!

"Article 30: Every year after every year, on the anniversary of this death that has happened to Us, the Nation has no right to celebrate on this day of Our death.

"Article 31: They must keep going to the front.

"Article 32: Economics is for donkies only. (Note: Bani-Sadr's Unitarian Economics is for Bani-Sadr only.)

"Article 33: They should not smite Islam in the visage.

"Article 34: They should not kick it up the backside either. (Note: This or that they must not do.)

"Article 35: But however, I shall not name in this article those who did whatnot with Islam, with Ayatollah Kashani, God bless his soul.

"Article 36: Dr Mossadeq.

"Article 38: This article is No. 38. Imam Khomeini.

"Article 37: But however, these two articles have been swapped.

"Article 39: The martyr Motahhari was a part of this dead body, he was.

"Article 40: Economics is for cows.

"Article 41: In the Tabas Desert, it was God's order to down those American helicopters.

"Article 42: And that dog who sniffed out that other plot, God's envoy that dog was.

"Article 43: But however, everybody thought that Bani-Sadr had uncovered it or Kianouri, bless his soul, had.

"Article 44: These conspiratorisors We have executed

were wild animals. (Note: Now *they* think *we* are wild animals.)

"Article 45: Torture not the innocent in jails.

"Article 46: But however, the 8-point Decree that We issued to the Nation, no one was heedful to it, maybe perhaps to this Will someone will be heedful instead.

"Article 47: Ahmad must copy this will ten times as his penance.

"Article 48: That's enough."

(signed) Notrouhollah al-Moussavi al-Khomeini al-Stiff

23 July 1983

Dear Doctor

Last week we announced that because a number of physicians who have recently fled Iran are contributors to Asghar Agha, *our readers can write to us about their medical problems. Should the problem be considered of a general nature, they would receive the reply through these same pages. What follows is the first such letter.*

Dear Sir,

I am an Iranian male. In my youth, I used to have acne. I wrote about that to the medical columnist of the *Weekly Ettela'at* magazine, and the acne disappeared gradually. Of course, they never answered my inquiry in that magazine!

After a while, I developed an ugly habit, which I was too embrarrassed to discuss with a doctor. So, this time I wrote to the *Youth* magazine's medical column and cryptically told them about my problem. A few weeks later they answered that I should do a little exercise, read books, keep my mind busy and try not to remain alone. I did all of that and it worked. A couple of years later I got married, and both the acne and that habit left me.

But now, with a wife and three kids, in a foreign land, I am facing another problem and, once again, I am too embarrassed to see a psychiatrist. I would therefore like to ask you to advise me in writing, but allusively, and of course referring only to my pen-name. Also, I'm writing this letter in a very bad hand-writing, because should my secret be revealed in any way, it would lead to the disruption of my family and to other painful consequences, consequences which I am as unable to explain as I am incapable to treat my illness.

And now my problem. At 48 years of age, with a wife and three children (and recently one daughter-in-law and one grandchild), having experienced one revolution, and having been active in the developments that led to the reinstatement of Dr Mossadeq in 1952 and in the events culminating in Dr Mossadeq's fall in 1953, and with a fair degree of political consciousness, I find myself unable to...treat my acne? No, sir. Get rid of that ugly daily habit? No, my dear fellow. I find myself unable to chose the future government of my country!

In all honesty, I am confused. I am perplexed. My head is boiling inside! Of my children, one is a Muslim socialist Mojahed; another is on the left, a Fadayee guerrilla; and the third calls himself a member of Allah's Party. My daughter-in-law is a fanatic Muslim who covers her hair even in front of her new-born son, but at the same time is an implacable enemy of Khomeini and the Islamic Republic. Because her father was a member of the Tudeh Party, my wife leans a bit toward Moscow and believes that if the Tudeh Party does not succeed in seizing power, all rights should be reserved for the Shah's eldest son Reza Pahlavi, as Reza Shah the Second, and no other group should have the right to form a government.

As for myself I am neither attracted by this, nor intimidated by that. I have neither become infatuated with this group, nor intoxicated with that one. Instead, I have been studying intensely. I want to know and to decide consciously. I will not tell you whether at the beginning I was or was not a supporter of Khomeini. Also, I did not make it clear what I did and which side I was on during the events of 1952 or those days in August 1953. It does not matter. I do not want to prejudice your mind. I would like to know what I am supposed to do today.

You see, my studies so far suggest the following options to me: Constitutional Monarchy, and Republic. The constitutional option has two branches: Shahollahism and monarchism. Shahollahism itself has two branches: Supporting the reign of Reza Pahlavi or supporting the reign of the late Shah's younger son, Ali-Reza Pahlavi. Supporting Reza Pahlavi as king would lead you down one of two paths: Condemning Mohammad-Reza Shah or condoning him. Supporting the reign of Ali-Reza Pahlavi too would leave you with a choice between two options. On the one hand, you could call for the formation of a Regency Council made up of the late Shah's twin sister, Ashraf Pahlavi, former Queen's Chief of Staff, Dr Nahavandi, and Mrs Maryam Firouz, the wife of Tudeh Party First Secretary Mr Noureddin Kianouri. (I have included the latter in the Regency Council because of my good lady's insistence; my missus too is, after all, a member of this amorphous opposition and believes that Mrs Firouz will eventually join the monarchist camp.) The other form of support for Ali-Reza Pahlavi's rule is to get him to issue a New Year message deposing his brother and declaring himself king.

Let us now consider the republican option. First of all, a republican regime could be one of the following two: theocratic or secular. As a secular republican, you will be faced with two choices: following the Shah's last Prime Minister, Dr Bakhtiar, and his Movement of National Reistance, or opposing Bakhtiar and forming a separate movement of national resistance (my wife says we should call it Movement of National Reluctance). As far as the theocratic republic is concerned, again at first sight there are two types: Marxist and non-Marxist. The non-Marxist theocratic republic can either be a national republic or a popular republic, or a mixture of national and popular republics, of the sort Admiral Madani has recently proposed. And the Marxist-theocratic republic is the sort that the Mojahedin want to set up, so that their regime would have the best of both worlds!

It should also be mentioned that in the secular republic category there are other regimes as well, such as Chinese communism, Albanian and even Russian communism and Islamic Fidel Castroism. Neither should one forget the existence of people's democratic republics, democratic people's republics, northern democratic people's republics, southern democratic people's republics, as well as other variations on this theme and, of course, the supporters of our 1906 Constitution!

In short, I do not know what to do. Because recently

another group, who call themselves old Dr Amini's Selfless Guerrillas, have started sending me their publications, but my wife says someone must be playing a practical joke on us!

We sit around day and night, reading the opposition literature. We cut out of the newspapers the various forms of government that are suggested and then, later at night, like children solving a jigsaw puzzle, my wife and I put our newspaper cuttings on the table, look at them, and rearrange them. My wife says, "This piece should go there", and I say, "That piece should go next to that other one, because both of them have to do with th same type of government." But no matter what we do, it doesn't work out. In the end the wife and I get into a row, crumple the newspapers and go to bed hoping for a better day tomorrow.

Dear Doctor! I am a practical person. I am neither an intellectual, nor would I vote for someone blindly. (Perhaps that's because I am not an intellectual.) I want to read, I want to know, and then decide. I read four books and half a dozen articles on the merits and drawbacks of separation of religion and politics, and it was only then that I learned that there were two sides to the issue. One being the separation of religion from politics and the other the separation of religion from state. Foolish me! Until then I had thought these two meant the same thing. My wife says religion should be separate from state but not separate from politics, because the Prophet has said, "Politicking is next to Godlicking!" I think there must be something wrong with this quotation that my wife cites. But I do not know Arabic.

It shouldn't go unmentioned that I take great interest in intellectuals. For example, I do not understand Shamlou's poetry, but I do very much like Dr Gholam-Hossein Saedi's plays, especially the one in which the great actor Entezami had a role. I have also read most of the articles written by Dr Haj-Seyyed-Javadi, because my grandfather too comes from the town of Qazvin.

When the intellectuals came from Tehran and joined the National Council of Resistance abroad, and there was no longer any intelllectual in Iran who had not left the country to join the Council, I was very optimistic. But when they began quarrelling among themselves over censorship, I too was very sad, because I like Ms Homa Nateq, like my own sister.

Dear Doctor! I swear by God that in my adolescent days, when I wrote about my acne to the *Weekly Ettela'at*'s medical advisor, I never offered so much detailed explanation. or for that matter, about that ugly habit of mine, I wrote only two lines to the *Youth* magazine's medical advisor, and he answered that I should exercise and try not to remain alone.

Now that I have filled most of a 20-page writing tablet— my wife's household accounts book—with the details of my condition with respect to the beloved homeland's future government, I would like to ask you to give me a few lines of advice in the next issue of *Asghar Agha*. Also, please let me know if medical magazines like *Medicine and Medication*, the *Medical World* and the *Family Doctor* are still published in Iran and if they publish something about the future regime. If so, I could ask the wife's brother to send them to me from Tehran. Because as far as this problem is concerned, we wouldn't overlook any publication, not even *Asghar Agha*.

I apologise for having disturbed you and having taken your time. You see, I didn't know of any alternative but you. I hope you don't misunderstand me. By referring to you as the "alternative", I did not mean that your good self, Mr Medical Advisor, would be Khomeini's successor. I meant to say that as far as I am concerned, and with respect to my medical problem I had no other alternative. This word "alternative" these days has acquired a very peculiar meaning.

In those very first days when the word "alternative" had become fashionable, I racked my brains until I understood what it meant. My wife used to tell me that in German "alternative" meant "Mojahedin". (We live in a German-speaking country.) Until one day I saw that the periodical *Iran and the World* was referrring to Reza Pahlavi as the "alternative"! My wife said: "See? Reza Pahlavi has also joined the Mojahedin!" But I didn't give up and made extensive studies about the meaning of the word "alternative", I even looked it up in several dictionaries, and at last I discovered that it had nothing to do with the Mojahedin and that even my wife could be an "alternative"! In my opinion, at present, if we can get hold of an Alternative Democratic Republic, or an Alternative National Republic, our country would be saved from its state of chaos, and I too would be saved from my state of confusion. Because at present what our country needs is first of all, raw materials for industry and, second, a strong alternative republic!

Dear Doctor! At the conclusion of my letter I have to disclose a bitter fact, namely that at the age of 48, with a wife and three children and recently one daughter-in-law and one grandchild, in a foreign land, because of my extensive studies on the merits and drawbacks of monarchy, the various types of republic, as well as rightwing, and middle-wing governments, and because I feel that as each day passes I move one step further away from the beloved homeland and I still haven't been able to make up my mind, recently I have once again been suffering from facial acne and, what's worse, because of my craving for the overthrow of the mullahs' government and my passion for the establishment of a healthy, democratic and popular government in the beloved homeland, that ugly habit of my youthful days has come back to me and sometimes, when I am alone, I am compelled to throw away all the opposition books, newspapers, magazines and bulletins and carry on with that ugly habit until the moment when a relative calm has subdued the flames that engulf my body. Unfortunately, the *Youth* magazine's advice cannot stop me from doing that either. I am most embarrassed to say that this is the only alternative that I have left. Please help me.

Sincerely yours, S.

Asghar Agha's Medical advisor replies:
Dear Mr or Mrs S.,
After reading your letter, I have now been hospitalised in one of London's most advanced hospitals.

Your Doctor
7 May 1983

The Eternal Struggle

One of the regime's propaganda ploys is to speak of plans that will take several years to be carried out. It appears that by outlining these plans they want to suggest that they will be in power for years to come and thereby discourage the opposition. (Do they really think our opposition would be discouraged so easily?)

The Prime Minister talks of a Five-Year Plan and the Minister of the Interior announces that people's identity cards will be replaced within eight years. The President has announced that "We will be self-sufficient in 12 years", and the Majlis Speaker has sketched a 20-year development plan.

It is not clear how a regime that we expect to fall within the next couple of weeks dares to make plans for the next 20 years!

Of course, the mullahs too have gotten it all wrong and do not know that the opposition is not sitting idly by in Paris. As soon as the Prime Minister speaks of the Five-year Plan, the opposition too, despite all its internal divisions, draws up its own five-year plan of struggle. And when the Interior Minister talks of eight years on, the opposition's plan is extended for another three, and just as Mr Rafsanjani refers to 20 years from now, the opposition draws up its plans of struggle for another 20 years.

In short, as long as this regime is in power, the opposition is not going to stop fighting even for a moment and, God willing, Khomeini's regime and the Paris opposition will carry on alongside each other, like two parallel lines, until eternity.

4 June 1983

PART THREE

IN WHICH nothing
quite works out...
(1982 till Lord, how long?)

Not an Interview with Jackie Kennedy

One fruit of our glorious Revolution is, indeed, the emergence of our Islamic magazine, Fundamentalist Woman, *to replace that ungodly rag,* Modern Woman, *which used to be published by the infidel Shah's lackies.*

In Fundamentalist Woman *we not only inform our readers of issues as diverse as the latest fashions in designer veils and how to get on with your husband's other wives, but we also keep them abreast of the exciting goings-on in the privacy of the homes of the Nation's leaders, men who have suddenly emerged from oblivion and are determined to take the whole country back there with them.*

Assisting us in this latter, vital task is Oriental ''Orie'' Fallacy, who has spent many hours interviewing the wives of brother ministers and other officials with such perception and, at the same time, such awe and affection that it would no doubt be the envy of many an infidel hackette. Jacqueline Kennedy would have been proud to have been interviewed by Orie. But, it was not to be. For Allah, the Compassionate, the Merciful says: ''And the Muslim reporteress shall not interview pagan women—let alone pagan men.

And, indeed, that is how it should be. And, indeed, that is how it was, as you shall see in the following searching look into the life and times of Baji Zobeydeh Rainollahi-Candlezadeh, the wife of

Mr Seyyed-Rezaoddin Rainollahi-Candlezadeh, the Minister of Water and Power of the Islamic Republic.

It was four in the afternoon when we entered the house of Mr Seyyed-Rezaoddin Rainollahi-Candlezadeh, the Minister of Water and Power. Baji Zobeydeh, the wife of Mr Seyyed-Rezaoddin Rainollahi-Candlezadeh, received us quite informally and warmly. A very intimate and personal welcome. As if she were not indeed the wife of Mr Seyyed-Rezaoddin Rainollahi-Candlezadeh, the Minister of Water and Power of the Islamic Republic.

We enter the drawing-room. Baji Zobeydeh sits on the floor, cross-legged, next to an armchair, and motions me to sit in the armchair. But, witnessing that the wife of the Minister of Water and Power herself is sitting on the floor, I decide that I should reciprocate her modesty. I too sit cross-legged on the floor. Baji Zobeydeh gets up and fetches the fruit bowl from the top of the mantlepiece, puts it on the floor in front of me and sits on the armchair.

(You will have no doubt noticed, dear reader, that at this point Orie has been conned. She sat on the floor in response to Baji Zobeydeh's assumed modesty. But now she has ended up cross-legged on the floor, while Baji Zobeydeh is perched on top of the armchair. Experienced reporter that she is, Orie immediately thinks up a ploy to counter Baji Zobeydeh's manoeuvre. Watch carefully to see how it works—Ed.)

I look around. On the mantlepiece I see a picture of Martyr Rajaie, next to it a picture of Martyr Beheshti catches the eye, and there is a picture of Martyr Bahonar on the other side. Something is written on the margin of Martyr Rajaie's picture which I cannot read from here. I get up, approach the mantlepiece and read the writing in the margin of the picture. It says: "Before I am martyred, I would like to present this picture to my dear friend and militant brother-in-trenches, Mr Seyyed-Rezaoddin Rainollahi-Candlezadeh, the Minister of Water and Power. (Signed) Mohammad-Ali Rajaie."

Tears fill my eyes. I go back and sit in front of Baji Zobeydeh on an armchair. (I told you, didn't I?—Ed.) I ask Baji Zobeydeh: "Has living with a minister put a heavy responsibility on your shoulders?"

Baji Zobeydeh, still sitting on the armchair (The poor girl has become obsessed with the armchair—Ed.), says: "Well, Reza and I divide up the responsibilities. You know, living in an atmosphere full of responsibility, especially when one's husband is responsible for 36 million people's water and power, is at any rate a heavy responsibility. I feel the responsibility shoulder-to-shoulder with Reza."

"Does His Excellency the Minister of Water and Power tell you about his meetings with the Imam?" I ask Baji Zobeydeh.

Baji Zobeydeh is staring into the far horizon on the wall across the room. I can see one of her eyes through the gap in her veil. She moves about on the armchair and says: "Reza has one weekly meeting with the Imam. It's normally on Wednesdays, unless Reza is busy. He really loves His Eminence the Imam, when he comes back from a meeting with His Eminence, he is in a good mood. He usually plays with the children."

"What types of games does His Excellency the Minister of Water and Power play with the children?"

"All sorts of games. But he usually tickles them and then he himself falls about laughing!"

"No doubt you receive many phone calls," I put it to the wife of the Minister of Water and Power. "Who normally answers the phone?"

"Well, whenever Reza's at home, he answers the phone himself. But if he's not in, then that's a different matter. Sometimes people ring up to see how His Excellency the Minister is; they really care about the Minister. Sometimes they're so excited they even refer to the Minister's mother and sisters. But I know Reza's mother and sisters. They're a good family."

"Who does the shopping?"

Baji Zobeydeh gets up from the armchair, straightens her veil, sits back and says: "As far as little bits and pieces are concerned, like bread and all, sometimes when Reza's at home he puts his pyjama trousers on and pops down to the shops. He doesn't really approve of me going out. But whenever he's busy, I also nip out round the block and come back quickly."

"What do the children think about their father?"

"Well, the little Mostafa's just started talking, and whenever his dad comes home, he starts shouting: "Donkey daddy, donkey daddy!" But my little girl Zahra is ten years old, and she's better in terms of thinking and understanding things. She argues with Mostafa about whether their dad is or is not a donkey. My three eldest daughters have all gotten married and, thank Allah, their husbands too are loyal to the Revolution and faithful to the Imam. I've also got three daughters-in-law.''

''You mean your three sons have also gotten married?''

''Oh no! We've married off only one of our sons, but he's got three wives.''

''Tell me about yourself, your hobbies, your interests. About your marriage and what it means to you, and what you think of the process of the Islamic Revolution in the contextual framework of the international struggle for freedom.''

Baji Zobeydeh has a quick reply: ''Well, it really depends. The day Reza came to ask for my hand, my father, God bless his soul, he said to me: 'Zobie, it's the goat that should decide if the grass is sweet or not.' That's the sort of school of thought that I've been brought up in.''

''Does His Excellency the Minister of Water and Power help you with the household chores, too?''

''Since he's become a minister he doesn't have the time. In the past, yes. But now, well now he's got a very heavy responsibility and can't do the washing-up like he did in the past. But of course there's always the Revolutionary Guards.''

''Does it ever make you feel tired, living with a minister?'' I ask Baji Zobeydeh.

''It depends on what sort of a minister, doesn't it?'' She asks rhetorically. ''I never wanted my husband to be Minister of Health or Minister of Justice, for instance. Let me tell you something: You might not believe this, but from the very first day, what I really wanted was this Ministry of Water and Power.''

"How do you get on with your relatives and friends?''

"It's all right, generally speaking. Since Reza's become
a minister I don't get to go and see them like I used to.
They often come here, but leave before Reza comes back,
'cause he must have some peace of mind at home.''

Baji Zobeydeh talks wisely and eloquently, but, alas, our
time is up. I gather from Baji Zobeydeh's tone of voice that
we must go now. Some foreign journalists are waiting in
the corridor with their cameras and microphones. We bid
farewell to Baji Zobeydeh. She gets up from the armchair,
sees us off to the door of the room, and we leave the wife
of Mr Seyyed-Rezaoddin Rainollahi-Candelezdeh, the
Minister of Water and Power of the Islamic Republic.

As we are leaving the room, I notice a huge picture of
our Great Leader Imam Khomeini on the mantlepiece,
between the pictures of Martyr Rajaie and Martyr Beheshti.

(Good job Orie saw that picture. Without a single word
about the Imam's picture in the whole interview, we'd have
ended up in the doghouse.—Ed.)

22 May 1982

It Didn't Quite Work Out—1

The egg, though hoping to become a chicken, ended up in an omelet, perhaps in the same omelet eaten, along with many other things, by one of the faithful one doleful Ramadan evening.

There was a time when we had casualties only in car crashes along the Haraaz Highway in those mountain stretches north of Tehran. (Well, not "only", really. I should have said mostly.) There was also a time when getting killed along the Haraaz Highway was the most natural type of death. Nowadays, everybody gets killed on the path of Islam.

There were frequent avalanches along the Haraaz Highway, and in fact there was also an avalanche along the path of Islam. But only once, in the winter of 1979.

I personally was for some sort of change. Some sort of transformation. Hoping for a deliverance, without knowing what shape it might take.

My life had remained untouched for years. No matter what I did, it would not change. I kept replacing my car, but still nothing really changed. So I thought, now that I can't change my life all on my own, maybe I should hope for something that would change everybody's life. So it was that I joined Khomeini's great call, the chorus of "All Together".

I was tolerating the presence of people whom I had hated all my life. Why? The first reason was that I could see that people who had hated me all their lives were smiling at me and were tolerating my presence.

I hated that life and life-style. All lies, total deception, complete corruption. I felt that I couldn't catch up with others in any of those fields. Others must have felt the same way towards me, and that must have been the reason why everybody poured out into the streets. I, of course, was on the sidewalk. But what difference did it make? There was no room on the streets. In fact the streets and the sidewalks had merged, like so many other things that had merged and could not be distinguished from each other.

I still don't wish I had been killed along the Haraaz Highway or that I had not seen what I had seen. No, I don't. I'm even very happy to have seen many things myself. Of course, I must be imagining that I have seen them, because sometimes I do things or say things as if I'd never seen any of that with my own eyes. Like so many others.

One day we were driving north to the Caspian coast in a little Paykan. Along the Haraaz road. They used to say the Paykan's engine would boil over when going uphill. But that wasn't true. Those were rumours spread by the Shah's enemies. At any rate, my Paykan would boil over when going downhill.

The story I'm telling you is about the days before that

omelet. It has to do with the days when the egg still had dreams of becoming a chicken. And what an egg it was! They used to say it had two yolks, but it hardly even had one. I heard it over the television myself. It was on the Evening News. The newsreader announced that according to the latest reports, all the eggs in the country had developed two yolks! I can remember it very well. I can remember exactly what the newsreader looked like. He was a gentleman with greyish hair, wearing a light blue necktie, with red, yellow and orange stripes. You do remember, don't you, that in those days we had colour television?

Near Aab-Ali (we were going along the Haraaz road) a friend said, "Let's go over to the Casino!" He meant the Aab-Ali Casino. I said I didn't feel like it. "Let's vote," he said. We did. There were two against, five for. (I don't know how we had managed to stuff seven people into a Paykan.) I was one of the opposition. So, having voted democratically, we didn't go to the casino! It's true that only me and another guy were against, but I was after all the driver.

Of course, if I could then have foreseen that one day they would close down the casinos, I would certainly not have disagreed with my friends' suggestion. But the way things were going, I used to think that if one day anything at all did happen, they would only close down the Aab-Ali yoghourt-drink bottling factory, and would leave the casino alone.

When we got to Babolsar on the Caspian coast and arrived at some friends' place, opium was sizzling on the pipes over the charcoal brazier. The sight of the charcoal, glowing on a bed of ashes like the jewels Nader Shah brought home from India, was enough to turn any junky into a poet or any poet into a junky.

We had barely finished our first round when a political discussion started. The friends from Babolsar were talking about their mayor and those of us from Tehran were complaining of Tehran's mayor. In those days we used to call such talk "political discussions"! It was later on—after the egg had been well beaten—when we had to smoke fake opium around the brazier, that I realized what real political debate was, though the other stuff was real enough back then in Babolsar. So we are condemned always to have something out of sinc. Either our politics or our opium.

Now when they say that "religion is the opium of the people," I wonder what type they're talking about. If religion is like that majestic stuff we smoked in Babolsar, then so much the better for the masses. But if it is going to be the rubbish that stretches like chewing gum, well, then I'd rather be a non-believer and go to Babolsar (the Babolsar of old).

I have had a close look at Marx. I've searched for the statement "religion is the opium of the people", but I haven't found it. It is difficult to find just one sentence in so many thick volumes. I wanted to write under it: "And Marx is the opium of the intellectuals." (I should have explained in a footnote that of course this phrase is not mine, and that I read it somewhere. But since footnotes and numbers in the middle of a text are like boulders along a road, and since I don't like to throw the reader up and down along the way, I'll make do with these brackets.)

In my lifetime, I have smoked opium only a few times. In fact, about five or six times. I have prayed about the same number of times. But fortunately I have neither become an opium addict, nor a practising believer. There are many who, after just one smoke, become opium addicts and have their lives ruined by it. But I did not imagine that from those ashes, or from the smoke inhaled through the opium pipe, or from the smoke I puffed up from my chest I would find what I was "missing".

Perhaps if I had been a true believer, I could have found it through prayer, but then again, the problem was that I didn't know how many times I would have to bend and bow in order to find it. I finally found what I was "missing" when I went out to search for it on the streets. And then it was like looking for a needle in haystack, because for reasons unknown to me, all the other people had chosen that same day to search for what they were missing.

A few days before that march, I had broken a window of our local bank with a brick. A window with which I had established an "emotional-metaphorical" relationship. My bus stop was opposite the bank and very often as I was waiting for the bus, I would look at my reflection in the bank's window. I would straighten my necktie, brush my hair with my fingers. Sometimes I used to think I had a date with myself. I would go there, and we would keep looking at each other until the bus arrived.

Now I don't know what came over me that made me smash up that full-length window pane. There were about a dozen of us. We neither knew each other, nor had a date to meet up, but for some mysterious reason had ended up together. I don't know where they had turned up from or how I had managed to get mixed up with them. We were throwing, breaking, burning things and moving on. And, of course, shouting slogans all the time. It was in the middle of all that commotion that I aimed a brick at the bank window. Why, I don't know. There was a crashing noise and my reflection fell to bits on the floor of the bank. A film of this episode would have to use slow motion to show how the slivers of glass turn in the air and how my pale reflection changes.

My mates climbed in and took the Shah's picture off the wall, and we burned it on the sidewalk. Oh how good that felt! I still don't regret having done it. But I wish there were someone in the world who could tell me why I broke the window. (Yes, to *tell* me, not to *ask* me.)

Someone with a television camera was following us all the while, filming what we were doing. It was as if we were doing all that for his benefit. He was a foreigner. Then another foreigner came along and stood by the fire and started talking into the microphone, also looking into the camera. It turned out they were from the BBC.

9 February 1985

Exclusive: Interview with Oil Minister Petrollahi

As the Islamic Republic News Agency's London correspondent, most of my time is taken up with making video recordings of the latest episodes of *Dallas* and *Dynasty* and sending them over to Tehran for the Majlis Speaker, brother Rafsanjani. But a few weeks ago, something very exciting happened. I heard that on his way from the OPEC meeting in Geneva, our country's Oil Minister, brother Petrollahi was going to stop over in this satanic island to attend the religious-political Friday Prayers services at the Imam Khomeini Prayer-and-Sports Complex on Kensington High Street.

As soon as I heard of brother Petrollahi's plans, I decided to take my chances and try to get him to give me an exclusive interview. Luckily, I ran into brother Petrollahi, just a few hours before he was due for the Friday Prayers, at the halal meat kebab take-away next to the Imam Khomeini Complex. Half a dozen sandwiches and fifteen Cokes later, brother Petrollahi kindly accepted my request.

Q. Would you please begin with a brief account of your struggles and how you became the Oil Minister?

A. In the Name of Allah, the Compassionate, the Merciful. Hail to the Great Leader of the Revolution and salute to the martyr-rearing Nation and hail and glory to the infidelity-fighting soldiers of Islam who are battling against eastern and western arrogance, led by the world-predator America, and its zionist agents such as the infidel Saddam Yazid and the other reactionary Arab sheiks and rulers. And curse and damnation, in alphabetical order, to Amini, Bakhtiar, Bani-Sadr, Madani and Rajavi, who are backed by the zionist, imperialist Mitterrand regime.

Before the Revolution, because of my fight against the Shah's regime, SAVAK agents prevented me from carrying on with my advanced studies into the skills of reading and writing at the Supreme Elementary School for Adult Education. As a result, myself and brother Tondgouyan, who is now in the hands of the zionist Saddam, had to spend sometime in secret unemployment.

Then we developed an interest in oil because we used to live next door to a petrol station and, in order to help the progress of the Revolution, we would go there every night and siphon off some petrol from the pumps.

After the traitor Shah fled the country and preparations were being made for our Uncompromising Imam's return to our Islamic homeland, since there was a possibility that the Imam's plane might run out of fuel, brother Tondgouyan and I loaded some ten gallons of high octane into the back of a van we had confiscated from someone we did not know but had good reason to believe he did not really need it, and drove towards the airport.

Fortunately, since Allah has always been on the side of

our Islamic Revolution and revolutionaries like myself, the Imam's plane had enough fuel and on the way back from the airport, brother Tondgouyan and I managed to sell our petrol reserves, at four times the price set by the infidel Shah's regime, to some people who had queued up outside our local service station.

Q. Speaking of oil price fluctuations, what do you think of OPEC and the efforts by the reactionary Saudi leaders to raise the price of oil?

A. Once again, hail to the Indefatigable Leader of the Great Islamic Revolution, who is on his way to save all the down-trodden peoples of the world.

At the last OPEC meeting in Geneva, the capital of our friendly neighbour, Italy, by the beautiful Lake Victoria, the accursed Yamani wanted to increase the price of oil. I realised immediately that this was a plot jointly concocted by the world-predator America and the Russian imperialists who are sucking the blood of the Muslim people of Afghanistan, with the aim of preventing us from selling more oil on the international market, getting all their dollars out of their pockets and driving them bankrupt.

So I charged towards Yamani, grabbed him by the neck and told him that he was nothing but an al-idiot and an al-nasty beast and that he should be ashamed of his al-goatee. Of course, being an agent of western arrogance, he does not understand Arabic well, but witnessing my wrath, he more or less got the message and left the conference hall to tell the imperialist and zionist media that the meeting had ended in failure.

19 February 1983

Living in Darkness
A Practical Guide by Ayatollah Montazeri

Introduction

In the Name of Allah, the Compassionate, the Merciful. First of all, is there anything wrong with darkness? Who could ever say that? Does the foetus in the womb carry a light? Was there a light on in your own mother's tummy when you were a baby, or in our neighbour's wife's tummy when I was still an unborn baby? Well of course not! The foetus is formed in the dark. The father and mother first turn off the lights and then say, "In the Name of Allah". Now, how is it that some people who haven't got electricity or who have long power cuts allow themselves to protest against the government? Do you think this is like the Shah's time? No, dear ones, we've still got a long way to go.

Now, back to our Practical Guide. There is nothing that can't be done in the dark. You've only got to have the know-how. The science of darkness is a very useful branch of knowledge, so you'd better listen carefully as we go along.

1. *How to eat a watermelon in the dark:*

This is really easy. You first cut it up and then eat it. As for the pips, since you can't remove them in the dark, you should swallow them. They won't go very far.

2. *How to eat a banana:*

There's nothing easier than eating a banana in the dark. Hold on to its tip, pull the skin off, and now your banana is ready to eat. It is, however, better to eat the skin first, because you might not feel like eating it afterwards.

3. *How to find a box of matches:*

According to His Reverance Imam Khomeini's *All You Never Wanted to Know About Sex With Animals and Other Subjects*, and as mentioned in other books, should one hold a box of matches near one's ear and shake it, one would hear it say: "Blessed are the matches in a box that is shaken near a believer's ear." So, if you happen to touch a small box while you are in darkness at work or in the kitchen at home, you should shake it near your ear. If it makes a noise, then it's a box of matches. If it doesn't make a noise, you should have your ears examined.

4. *How to tell twins apart:*

Let us assume that you have a pair of twins whose voices you cannot distinguish from each other. In the dead of the night one of them starts crying because he wants to be taken out for a wee. They're sleeping next to each other, and you can't tell which one is crying. Put your hand on their tummies, one at a time, and press hard. If the baby starts to cry louder, then that is the one you should take out. Similarly, when you are holding the baby on the toilet, if you notice that it has four legs, you can tell that you've got Siamese twins.

5. *Telling a spoon from a fork:*
Unfortunately, spoons and forks are quite similar as far as their tails are concerned. Therefore, you should examine their front parts. Rub your hand on the tip of the fork/spoon. If it is smooth, then you've got a spoon in your hand. However, should it later turn out to be a fork, then its tip must have been rather rough. To be double sure, hold the fork/spoon by the tail and press its tip on the palm of your hand. If it won't go in, you've got a spoon in your hand, but if it does go in, then it's probably a knife.

6. *How to drink tea:*
   In order to pour tea in the dark, hold the teapot very carefully by its handle, move it as close to the teacup as you can and then pour. If your teacup won't fill up, it's probably because it is upside down. Turn the cup round with your free hand and repeat the exercise. This time you are bound to fill your teacup unless, of course, you are holding the teapot by its spout.

7. *How to fasten a zip:*
   In order to fasten your zip, act as you would in the light. That is, pull up the small metal handle on the zip and it will fasten automatically. If the metal handle does not move, no matter how hard you pull it, you can conclude that your zip is already fastened.

8. *How to drive a nail into a wall:*
   If you need to drive a nail into the wall in order to hang a blessed picture of Imam Khomeini in your room, you should hold the nail against the wall and bang it with a

hammer. If it doesn't go into the wall, it's probably because you are holding it the wrong way round. Keep the nail in the same position, but move across the room and try to drive it into the opposite wall.

9. *How to sit cross-legged on the floor:*

Sitting down cross-legged in the dark is a most difficult exercise. In order to guide your feet, tie a piece of rope to each of your big toes. Then sit down on the floor. Hold the right toe-rope with your left hand and the left toe-rope with your right, passing one rope over the other in the process, and pull both ropes very hard. If the ropes don't break, your feet will soon be in their proper places and you'll be sitting cross-legged.

23 July 1983

Rafsanjani Reassures

Majlis Speaker Hojatoleslam Hashemi-Rafsanjani has denied the Iraqis' claims that they have sunk several Iranian vessels in the Persian Gulf. "When a missile is fired from a distance of 200 miles or more, it is bound to miss the target," Mr Rafsanjani explained, addressing last week's Friday Prayers congregation in Tehran.

This statement by the Supreme Defence Council spokesman has caused great relief in Moscow and Washington, where military officials now know they cannot be hit by the other side's missiles.

Heart-to-Heart with Sister Roqi

This week devoted readers of Fundamentalist Woman *accompany our ace reporter "Orie" Fallacy on yet another adventure as she interviews the better half of His Excellency the Minister of Emporial Affairs.*

I found our sister Roqieh, known to her closer acquaintances as Roqi, at the Ministry of Emporial Affairs. We had first gone to her house, but were told that sister Roqi was over at the Ministry.

When I and the sister photographer entered the Minister's suite, his secretary gave us a warm welcome. The way the brother Minister's secretary went about his duties was a model of how a believer-member of the Party of Allah works. Simultaneously he would type letters and answer several telephone calls.

Brother secretary told us there was no end of work. Working as the Minister's secretary, he said, wasn't his main job. He was called Feizollah. "Two weeks ago," he said, "they asked me to come and help here. Before that I used to be a shoe-keeper at the shrine of St. Ma'ssoumeh,

118

may peace be upon her."

I asked brother Feizollah about sister Roqieh. He told us she was in the Minister's office. Sister photographer and I entered the Minister's office. We were surprised to find sister Roqieh at the ministerial desk. She sensed that we were surprised.

"Reza," she said, affectionately referring to His Excellency the Minister, "he's gone out to buy a couple of hinges. You know, the hinges on our chest broke a few weeks ago. The brother Revolutionary Guards bought a hundred different types of hinges and they did a lot of work too, but none of those hinges fit our chest. In the end Reza said he'd go down the road himself and buy the hinges and told me to sit at his desk just in case someone came along with some business."

At this point sister Roqieh makes it clear that she is less than satisfied with the work she has been doing so far. "But none of the phones work, you know," she says with resentment. "I suspect they're connected to the secretary's office too, and this brother Feizollah likes to answer all the calls himself. I pleaded with him to let me have at least some of them, but he wouldn't."

I look around the Minister's office. Several large armchairs. On the mantlepiece, a picture of the Imam seated in an armchair. A chandelier with five 100-watt electric bulbs hanging from the ceiling. On one wall, several sockets and switches and over on the other side of the office, a blue globe. I give it a jab with my finger. It turns around several times and then stops by itself.

I sit on a chair facing sister Roqieh. I ask her what's new.

Sister Roqieh has covered her face so tightly I can hardly see even her eyes. "You're in the printing business," she says, "you've got all the news."

"How did you feel," I ask sister Roqieh, "when your husband Mr Prayerbookdealer was appointed Minister?"

"What did you say?" sister Roqieh cunningly asks.

I repeat the question and sister Roqieh, while cleaning the telephone with the corner of her chador, says: "Before Reza became a minister, Mr Candlezadeh had been appointed Minister of Water and Power. You see, he's one of our relations. His wife is the sister of my husband's sister-in-law. So when Mr Chandlezadeh got a job as a minister, Reza also started getting ideas and went over to see the Imam. But you're not going to print all this, are you?"

"But sister Roqi," I say in reply, "why should I not print the truth? Has the martyred Professor Motahari not said in his own book that we should publish the truth? Let the Muslim nation learn that there is a world of difference between how people became ministers under the previous ungodly regime, and how they are appointed now in the Islamic Republic."

"But of course," says sister Roqieh, "what I mean is that I don't want Mr Candlezadeh's wife to read all that. You see, she buys the *Weekly Ettela'at*."

"But I'm from *Fundamentalist Woman*."

"Well, it's all right then. You can ask whatever you want, but, God forbid, not the sort of questions that Radio Isreal could use in their programs."

"How many children do you have?" I ask sister Roqieh.

"Four. Four boys."

"Thank Allah for that! How do they get on with His Excellency the Minister?"

"Terribly," sister Roqi says with a sigh.

"What do you mean?"

"Well, you see, they'd like to kill each other."

"Why? What's the matter?"

"Well, you see," sister Roqieh says while lowering her voice, "these boys are not His Excellency the Minister's own children. I've got them from my previous marriage. That's why they're fighting each other like cats and dogs all the time. The other night, one of the boys tried to knife His Excellency. Thank God, the Minister's secretary was there and started swearing at the boy's father and mother like you'd never have heard, and then he slapped him a few times and the boy calmed down."

"Don't you and his Excellency the Minister have any children?"

"No, we haven't. He doesn't have the time. He's very busy. He's got one leg here in the Ministry and the other leg down at the hardware. One leg here and the other over at the builders' merchant. You see, we're tiling the floor of our living room. It's going to look great, just like the butcher's walls. It's much better than putting on wallpaper."

"Why don't you use carpets?" I ask.

"Later! You see, you've got to put on the tiles first, and then stick down the carpet on top of them."

I ask sister Roqi about His Excellency the Minister's private life. "He wouldn't even tell *me*," she says. "All I know is that every Wednesday he goes to the public baths.

Of course 'incognito', as they say, because..."

"Because he wants to be treated like other people, without any discrimination?"

"That's right. Otherwise, do you know how much the workers there would expect in tips? Even right now, he's gone incognito to buy us hinges."

"How do you feel when you come to the Ministry and sit at His Excellency the Minister's desk?" I ask sister Roqieh.

"I'm feeling a bit worried right now," she says, "because it's an hour and a half since Reza left. How long does it take to buy a few hinges? And especially when you're a minister? I'm really worried. I'm afraid, because he might be assassinated some time. Of course, he's got three body guards and with himself that makes four of them, and I can't imagine any terrorist would dare fight four body guards."

"Has His Excellency taken his bodyguards along?"

"No, he hasn't. He gave them the slip. They would've charged him three times as much for the hinges if he'd taken his bodyguards along."

We haven't got much time left. I tell sister Roqieh that we have to leave. Moving about on the Minister's swivel chair, sister Roqieh kindly asks us to stay on. "What's the rush," she says, "I'm stuck here all on my own and haven't got anything to do."

Sister photographer informs us that she has run out of film. She has used two 24-exposure rolls already. But sister Roqieh comforts her: "Take your time," she says, "Reza'll be here in a moment and I'll send him over to the shops to buy you some more film." She then invites us to tea and expertly presses a button to call an aide. A door opens at the end of the office. A brother Revolutionary Guard enters, a rifle on his shoulder and a tray in his hands. "Will you get two cups of tea for the ladies, and some canned fruit for me, please?" she says without turning her face towards the brother Revolutionary Guard.

"We've run out of canned fruit," the brother Revolutionary Guard says selflessly. "I told His Excellency the Minister to get some on his way back to the office."

"That's why it's taken him so long," sister Roqieh says with a sigh. She then gets angry and tells the brother Revolutionary Guard not to bring any tea either! The brother Revolutionary Guard feels embarassed and leaves the room.

Our time is over. We bid sister Roqieh farewell. She sees us off to the elevator. We tell her to give our regards to His Excellency the Minister and tell him that the Nation is proud of him. In reply she tells us to press the lowest button in the elevator.

A few moments later the elevator has taken us down to the Ministry's ground floor. As soon as we leave the elevator, by the power of Allah its doors shut automatically.

5 June 1982

It Didn't Quite Work Out—2

In those days I could not understand why the BBC film crew were so interested in filming what we were doing. To tell the truth, it was the first time in my life that I was involved in a revolution. Of course, in my school days I had had several fights with the other boys. But I'd never before been in a full-scale revolution with fights all over the place, breaking windows and burning the Shah's picture. I had never played in the movies either.

Ever since I was a kid, I've always liked important-looking actors like Nasser Malek-Moti'i. I even saw him once at Saint Abdollah's Shrine, but I had never had any other artistic activity, and this was the first time I was seeing movie cameras close up. What's more, they were taking pictures of me.

Now, some six or seven years later, I'd love to see those films. I wish I could go to BBC archives in London to see all the films on the Iranian Revolution in order to find my own pictures and sit there, all eyes.

Of course, there is more to my revolutionary credentials than those few hours of wrecking and burning. I also had ties with the intellectuals, and I will never forget the poetry nights at the Goethe Institute. My cousin used to live nearby and that's why, wherever we were, we'd make sure to get there in the evening. I remember that one night a lady was reading some poetry. I thought she was Shams Aal-Ahmad! I mean, honestly, until then I didn't know Shams Aal-Ahmad was a man. I used to think that someone called Shams had to be a woman. The only thing I wasn't sure of was whether this Shams Aal-Ahmad was the sister or the widow of Jalaal Aal-Ahmad.

That night, when that lady read her poetry, I asked a gentleman sitting next to me whether she was Shams Aal-Ahmad. He looked at me strangely and muttered: "Stupid SAVAK agent!" I said I might be stupid, but I certainly wasn't a SAVAK agent. Just then the lady whom I had taken for Shams Aal-Ahmad finished reading her poetry, and a man came to the platform to announce that the next speaker would be Mr Shams Aal-Ahmad! Only then I realised that Shams Aal-Ahmad was after all a man! I felt really embarassed in front of the gentleman sitting next to me. I could now see why he had looked at me like that. I was sweating all over. I didn't know what to do. I looked in his direction through the corner of my eye. He wasn't there! When I looked up, I saw that he was on the platform! O my! I had got myself in such a terrible mess that I couldn't stay there a moment longer. I got up and left.

That night my cousin searched all over for me, and since he didn't find me, he thought SAVAK had gotten rid of me!

I frequently ask myself why I got involved in the Revolution. I sit in front of the mirror and try myself. I am no impartial judge, otherwise I would have had myself executed several times over by now.

No one taught me how to make a revolution. Among the politicians I knew only Daryoush Forouhar, because a few years back he beat up my cousin. I think it was at a box office queue in front of a cinema or somewhere. Anyway they'd gotten into a fight over whose turn it was, and as a result my cousin gets beaten up and goes home. You'd say, not much of an acquaintance, eh?

23 February 1985

Vote Making

By-elections are underway in Iran for the Majlis [Parliament] seats vacated by deputies who have lost their lives to assassins' bullets, because of careless driving in bullet-proof cars, or simply due to over-eating at public or private functions. To convey to you a feeling of this exciting day, here is a report from our fundamentalist correspondent in Tehran:

REPORTER: Right now I am standing in front of a polling station at the office of an Islamic Revolutionary Committee. Hezbollahi masses are expected to pour their votes into ballot boxes here, as well as everywhere else. As I am talking, I can see a member of the Hezbollahi masses emerging from his house and rushing towards the polling station at an incredible speed. I might just be able to have a short interview with him. Brother! Brother!

MAN: Yes, what is it?

REPORTER: Could I have a word with you, please?

MAN: Listen, I'm in a terrible rush. I've got to get inside the *Komiteh* as soon as possible.

—There is no need to hurry, brother. You still have

plenty of time to cast your vote.

—What vote? The toilet at my place is blocked and I want to use the one at the *Komiteh*.

—Do you really, brother? I thought you were going to vote.

—Have you seen anyone voting with a roll of toilet paper?

—Well, never mind. Can you tell me whom you are going to vote for, once you have come out of the toilet?

—Well, for the toilet itself, really, I think it's cleaner than all the candidates.

REPORTER (into the microphone): Dear listeners, I hope you have not been shocked by our friend's revolutionary sense of humour. He only meant to have a little joke. What is certain is that in a few minutes the Hezbollahi masses will swarm over to the polling stations. In fact, at this very moment I can vaguely see a figure some distance away. I must point out that this is one of the most heavily populated parts of the city and no doubt we shall soon see millions of people coming over here to vote. Yes, in the meantime the figure I had seen at a distance has come closer. It is still getting closer.... and closer.... and closer. Hello, brother!

SECOND MAN: Hello!

REPORTER: How will you cast your vote?

—SECOND MAN: What for?

—For the Majlis elections, obviously!

—Is it a free election?

—Why, of course it is!

—In that case, I would like to vote for Dr Bakhtiar, Dr

Amini, brother Rajavi and the young King Reza Pahlavi.

—Brother, what on earth are you talking about? Have you lost you mind?

—Didn't you say we were going to have free elections? And shouldn't there be an opposition in a free parliament? Well then, I want to vote for the opposition.

—Brother, I can see that your real intention is not to vote, but to commit suicide, in which case I suggest you go to the war front...

REPORTER: Dear listeners, it is now about twelve-thirty and here at the polling station a huge crowd of brothers from the Revolutionary Guards Corps, the Mobilised Downtrodden Volunteers Corps, and the Elections Supervision Headquarters are ready to welcome the waves of our Muslim Nation who are expected to come in and cast their votes. At this very moment the self-sacrificing Revolutionary Guard brothers are knocking on the doors of the houses in the area and advising their residents with respect to their participation in the elections.

I am right now witnessing a most inspiring spectacle: The Revolutionary Guard brothers are bringing in the first voter. Two Revolutionary Guard brothers are holding the voting brother's legs, and two other brothers, from the Mobilised Downtrodden Volunteers Corps, their arms entwined with the voting brother's, lead him towards the ballot box. The volunteer voting brother is chanting revolutionary slogans.

THIRD MAN (his voice becoming louder as he comes nearer): Let go of me, you sons of bitches! I don't want to vote!

REPORTER: Oops, I am sorry! We seem to be having a problem here. I will discuss this with the Revolutionary Guard brother who is leading this operation. Brother, why does this brother not want to vote?

GUARD: Well, it's not really that 'e don' wanna vote, you know. Trouble is, 'e says 'e's allergical to elections, on account of wot them used to do wot wi' riggin' the votes and all that, before this our glorious Islamic Revolution.

REPORTER: How do you deal with such a situation?

GUARD: We talk to 'em. We tell 'em this elections is free. Look! Look at 'im right now! That same bro'er that was bein' so difficult 'as now gone quiet an 'e's now putting 'is vote in. That's because the bro'ers have made 'im understand that these our elections is different wi' 'em old uns.

REPORTER: You are absolutely right. Dear listeners! I saw with my own eyes that the same volunteer brother who had to be dragged to the ballot box, overcame his bitter memories of the old, ungodly regime, willingly and happily cast his vote, and is now leaving the polling station. Let me have a short interview with him. Excuse me, brother! Can you tell me whom you have voted for?

VOTER: In the name of Allah, the Compassionate, the Merciful. I voted for the four brothers who so gallantly and chivalrously helped me find the correct path and discover the true spirit of the Islamic Revolution.

REPORTER: Dear listeners, I'm still in front of the polling station in this old neighbourhood which houses millions of

130

our revolutionary Muslim people. The Revolutionary Guard brothers have just now managed to help a second voter in and out of the polling station. The volunteer brother voter is now leaving, with a broken arm and traces of blood over his face. Excuse me, brother! Could you please say whom you voted for?

SECOND VOTER: In the name of Allah, the Compassionate, the Merciful. Hail to Imam Khomeini, Leader of the Islamic Revolution and Founder of the Islamic Republic of Iran. Hail to the combatants of Islam. Death to the heathen Saddamites. Death to America. Death to the Soviet Union. Death to Israel and all other agents of international arrogance. I voted for Ayatollah Blankollah.

21 April 1984

How to Block The Straits of Hormuz
A Do-It-Yourself Manual
By Ayatollah Montazeri

In the name of Allah, the Compassionate, the Merciful. As Hojatoleslam Hashemi-Rafsanjani has said, to block the Hormuz Straits, you only have to sink a 500,000-ton vessel right in the middle of the waterway. Just one 500,000-ton vessel. But how do we do that?

Well, it's easy enough. First you must weigh the ship. To do that, you must put the ship on the scale. If the scale proves to be too small, you need only cut the ship in half and weigh each half separately. And don't worry about wrecking the ship, because you won't be needing it any more, will you? You're going to sink it, so it doesn't really matter if it's a whole ship, or two halves of ship. You must ensure, though, that each half weighs exactly 250,000 tons.

Having weighed the ship, you now want to sink it. To do that, you need some glue to stick the two bits together. You then take the ship over to the river, I mean to the Straits of Hormuz, and simply push it out into the water. If it sinks at the first go, all the better. Otherwise, you might need to take it out onto the shore and push it back into the water again, as many times as necessary.

Now you have sunk the ship and blocked the Straits of

Hormuz. But let's suppose that after a few months Iraq, Giscard d'Estaing and Ronald Reagan have been punished enough and we want to take the ship out of the water and use it again. What do we do now? Again, it's all very easy. You only need a magnet weighing 750,000 tons, that is, one and a half times the weight of the ship. Remember, the weight of the magnet must always be one and a half times the weight of the ship you want to salvage.

And what should that magnet look like? Well, obviously it should be shaped like a horse-shoe. To produce such a magnet you need to take a horse over to the magnet factory, lift one of its legs—don't lift more than one leg because the horse might fall down—yes, I was saying, lift one of the horse's legs, take a good look at its shoe, and bend your magnet so it takes a similar shape. You then take the magnet over to the Persian Gulf, hang it by a rope over the Straits of Hormuz and lower it very gently, and before the magnet touches the surface of the sea, the ship will have been drawn up to the magnet, bang, like that.

Now your Straits are open and your 500,000-ton vessel is also ready to sail. There is, of course, one little problem, namely that the magnet is stuck to the ship and can't be separated from it. But that doesn't really matter, does it? You can let the ship take the magnet along wherever it goes. And what about the excess baggage charges one has to pay, you may ask? Well that I'm afraid, is something you have to put up with, because, as they say, there's no such thing as a free anti-imperialist struggle.

8 October 1983

Letter To Andropov

The True Story Of Haj Fazel Khaniabadi's Visit to Moscow, As Told For The First Time By Himself

As I was flipping through the newspapers, I came across a hot story: An American girl, called Samantha Smith, who had been invited to Moscow by Yuri Andropov, had just spent two weeks there as the Soviet government's guest and now, on her way back home, was stopping over in Germany to play in a movie.

The reason for Andropov's invitation had been a letter by the girl who had asked him to do something, for God's sake, to protect world peace. In his reply, Andropov had told her not to worry, and had said that since she was such a nice girl, she could go to Moscow with her mom and dad for fourteen days of fun, and after that she could become a movie star.

Once I'd read that story, I started getting ideas. I thought I'd pretend I was my ten-year-old son and write a letter to Andropov asking for world peace. Once we received the invitation, myself, the son and the wife would get on an Aeroflot Iluyshin 64, fly to Moscow, fill up with vodka and caviar and then go on to Germany. There, the son would become an actor and me and the wife would join the opposition, issue political statements and hold press conferences.

I talked this over with the wife and after three days' hard work we came up with this letter:

Dear Uncle Andy,

Hello. How are you? I hope you have recovered from your illness. In case you'd like to know how we are, I should most humbly say that, thank God, we are fine and are living happily in the Islamic Republic.

By the way, dear Uncle, the reason why I'm writing this letter is to ask you to please protect world peace, which is really only in your kind hands. Dear Uncle, please accept my request and protect world peace and, by the way, if you want to send an invitation for me and my mom and dad, please kindly book us seats next to the windows, because my dad would very much like to see Moscow from up there.

Thank you in advance for all the trouble you'll have to go through. Your nephew, Assdollah Khaniabadi, ten years old, Class 4-B, Shari'ati Elementary School, Mowlavi Street, Qanatabad, just before the former Execution Square.

The wife thoughtlessly said we should also pretend we're members of the Tudeh Party. And I thoughtlessly smacked her in the mouth so hard that I kept apologising for three days.

The next day I posted the letter to: "Moscow, Red Square, on the Right Hand Side, the Kremlin Palace, please deliver to Mr Yuri Andropov." I then went back home and told the wife to start packing, put an ad in the Islamic Republic daily saying we were selling our furniture

135

on account of going away, then pop into the local mosque and ask the mullah the exchange rate for the US dollar, pound sterling, German mark, or Russian rouble, and then buy a bottle of vodka from the *Komiteh* and come back. I myself went over to the local bookshop and bought a Russian phrase book, published by the People's Path Press, and returned home.

In the meantime, the wife had put the bottle of vodka on ice and had also prepared some yoghourt-and-cucumber. (All of this had cost only 1,400 toomans). I drew the curtains, sat in a corner of the room, poured myself a glass of vodka, said *nazdroiya khrasho* and knocked it back.

I then started appreciating how clever I was. With this trick I was playing on Andropov and the KGB, I was outsmarting all the world's conmen and was really giving it to the KGB, the Kremlin and the Communist Party's Central Committee, and that should make up for all they'd done to us. "Well done, man," I said to myself.

I poured myself another glass of vodka...and imagined I was walking about in Moscow, around Red Square. I'd get to a neat and cosy bar, with a Russian monsieur behind the counter. Who knows, this may well have been the same bar where Dostoyevski, Chekhov, Gogol, Mongol and in more recent times Anatoly Sharansky used to drop in to have a spot of vodka.

I'd go in, order a half bottle and a few slices of pickled cucumber and sit in a corner to have Russian fun. Who knows, right at this moment a Russian tart might walk in, wrap her arms around me and ask me in Russian if I have any chewing gum, nylon tights, scarves or Winstons...I'd say yes! Then we'e go somewhere cozier and she'd tell me, "*Yazeti bieh liublo,*" and I'd tell her "I loved her too."

It was some twenty days later when the wife rang me up and told me to rush home because a letter had arrived. I asked her where the letter had come from and she said from the Embassy of the Union of Soviet Socialist Republics. "God's truth?" I asked. "Why should I lie?" she answered. I didn't waste a moment. I closed the shop, hopped into a former 5-rials taxi (which nowadays costs 150 rials) went home, opened the letter and started reading:

Dear little Assdollah Khaniabadi, 10 years old,

This is to acknowledge receipt of the letter that your father wrote in your name. We read the letter and passed it on to Mr Andropov. You'll find enclosed Mr Andropov's reply in his own handwriting:

Dear Assdollah,

Please tell that scum of a father of yours he should be ashamed of himself for impersonating a ten-year-old child. Does he think Moscow is a public toilet, open for just any punk to walk in? Listen you arsehole, that guy we invited to come over here was first of all an American, secondly his kid's name was Samantha, not Assdollah. We told him to come over here so that we could show him some stuff he could actually talk about back home.

If you make a fool of yourself just once more, we'll send a heavy KGB agent over to give you such a kick up the ass that it'd break Rafsanjani's teeth. Then we'd tip you off to the Revolutionary Guards as a Tudeh Party member, just as we did with all the others. So be careful and try to learn a lesson from what happened to that poor sod Kianouri. He'd also decided he wanted to come back to Moscow.

Yours, Yuri Andropov

What News From Iraq?

According to Reuters, reporting from Baghdad, Iraqi weather forecasts are regarded as important strategic information and are kept as part of the country's military secrets. Our own special correspondent has managed to send the following detailed report on a recent trial at an Iraqi court. Readers will note the similarities to procedures at Iran's Islamic revolutionary courts:

JUDGE: Hossein Abdollah! You are charged with having made a weather forecast during the war. Do you have anything to say to defend yourself?

DEFENDANT: I did not make a weather forecast.

JUDGE: You are a lying scoundrel! Security agents have reported that you predicted the weather conditions and told your neighbour about it too.

DEFENDANT: No Sir, that is not true. It's just that my neighbour came over and suggested that we go on a picnic over the weekend. I said we could do that if, God willing, the weather is not bad.

JUDGE: Did you mean the weather could be bad?

DEFENDANT: No Sir, I did not mean that. I was only being prudent.

JUDGE: Ha! You call that "prudence"? At a time when our country is at war and when even some from the enemy camp supply us with military intelligence, you, an Iraqi citizen, make a weather forecast and announce it, and you call that "prudence"? That is the essence of imprudence! That is treachery itself!

DEFENDANT: Firstly, I did not announce anything. I only said it quietly to my neighbour. Secondly, there was nobody there, except me and my neighbour, to hear what I said. There were no agents there either and I do not know how a security agent could have heard it.

JUDGE: You fool! The security agent is your neighbour himself. Do you not know that one out of every eight Iraqi citizens is a security agent?

DEFENDANT: I know nothing about making weather forecasts, Sir. I am only a simple grocer. My neighbour says, How about going on a picnic over the weekend, and I said it all depended on the weather, and we had to pray to God for good weather.

JUDGE: Under the present conditions? May God damn your father's spirit! You commit treason, collaborate with the enemy, provide Iran with meteorological information, and then you have the nerve to say you have done nothing? Acting in the exalted name of our esteemed leader, His Excellency President Saddam Hossein, this military tribunal finds you, Hossein Abdollah, guilty of treason and collaboration and sentences you to life imprisonment.

DEFENDANT: Aren't you going to let my lawyer defend me?

JUDGE: Your lawyer himself has been sentenced to ten years' imprisonment. You can chatter for a while as your final defence.

DEFENDANT: You are trying Hossein, son of Abdollah, but I am Abdollah, son of Hossein. I believe there has been a mistake.

JUDGE: There has been no mistake. You should thank God that you are Abdollah, son of Hossein. Had you been Hossein, son of Abdollah, we would have executed you already.

11 January 1986

It Didn't Quite Work Out—3

Perhaps one of our misfortunes in Iran was the over-supply of intellectuals. A shortage of navvies, but an abundance of intellectuals. All the navvies had become intellectuals. They'd each buy a copy of *Ferdowsi* magazine and in the evenings they'd walk along Naderi Street in central Tehran, go to cafés to have tea, coffee, beer or vodka, or a mixture of all of them, and exchange revolutionary winks.

I myself was an intellectual for a few weeks—all for the price of a magazine. At the beginning when I wasn't really into it, I didn't know that to be an intellectual you had to buy *Ferdowsi*, which was named after our 10th-century poet. I used to think I could buy *Rowshanfekr (The Intellectual)*. A couple of times I walked along Naderi Street with a copy of *Rowshanfekr* in my hand and had a few beers in the cafés, but none of the intellectuals would pay any attention to me. All the same, I'd sit there and read at my leisure.

After a while, when I had looked around more carefully, I realised that I had been misled by the name of the magazine, and the one which would give me the status of intellectual was *Ferdowsi*, not *The Intellectual*! It's true what

141

they say, that "the bird that will eat figs must have a crooked beak." But my beak had apparently been a bit too crooked.

One day my cousin came to me and said: "Why is it that in the intellectual circles they call you a SAVAK agent?" "Where are these intellectual circles?" I asked. "The Naderi Café, the bar across the road from it, and a few other spots along Naderi Street," he answered. I said that I hadn't shown them my SAVAK membership card, and in fact I didn't have one to show them anyway, and that I hadn't shown anyone anything except a magazine, *The Intellectual*, which I had taken there to read. "That's bloody it, then!" he snapped. I asked if *The Intellectual* was published by SAVAK. "No," he said, "but these people, if they see any other magazine except *Ferdowsi* in your hand, will think you're a SAVAK agent."

From then on, I would buy *Ferdowsi* and go to Naderi Street. But then I heard they were saying behind my back that I was an undercover SAVAK agent and that's why I was now buying *Ferdowsi*, rather than *The Intellectual*. In such an atmosphere you can see how difficult it was not to be a SAVAK agent! When I heard these gossipy intellectuals were tittle-tattling like that behind other people's backs, I decided to give up being an intellectual forever. One day when I had hired a copy of *Ferdowsi* (real intellectuals wouldn't buy the magazine, they'd rent it), I tore it up and chucked it into the gutters of Naderi Street and by doing so effectively announced my resignation from the ranks of the intellectuals to all the passers-by.

I once knew a talented young man who used to write

poetry. He was a nice fellow who had just come from the country. He was in touch with the intellectuals, but he had not yet become addicted to heroin. He made friends with me, perhaps only so that he could come read his latest poems to me. He wasn't much of a pretty boy, but still he swore by his mother that one of Naderi Street's intellectuals had designs on him and in order to promote his desires had agreed to write an introduction for his book of poems. "The son of a bitch," the young man would say, "he thinks he can do that with an introduction." "Well," I said, "if he wanted to do it without an introduction, you wouldn't find it so nice either!"

On another occasion this same young man invited me to have a kebab from one of the shops on Qavamsaltaneh Street. Afterwards out on the sidewalk he put his hand in his pocket and pulled out a piece of paper. "More poems?" I asked. "Not on your life," he said. "This here I want to read to you is worth all the poems that me, Shamlou and Nossrat Rahmani have written and all the books written by Aal-Ahmad, Saedi and the others put together."

"What is it then?" I asked. He took me away to a deserted, dead-end alley and, frightened and trembling, began reading to me. "This is a statement by Ayatollah Khomeini," he first said. "It asks why women have been given the right to vote. For God's sake, just listen to what he's got to say. It's really moving. Really moving."

As he was quaking and shaking, he read the whole statement to me. I didn't know how I should react. I didn't know what an intellectual was supposed to do when faced with such a statement. I was afraid that he might be teasing me. I was worried that I might discredit myself totally in all the intellectual circles. "Will you give me a copy of that?" I asked. "I'll give you a thousand and one," he said. "Throw the thousand into people's houses and keep one for yourself."

Never mind what I did, but that budding revolutionary poet was executed two years after the glorious Islamic Revolution. Now, if he had been executed because of being a poet, or because of a particular work he had written, he might have fulfilled his ambition of a mention in the press as a poet. But it was on charges of drug-smuggling that they put that innocent kid in front of the firing squad. Now, with this regime, you shouldn't really be surprised if some time they execute drug-traffickers on charges of writing poetry.

16 March 1985

Friday Prayers At Hyde Park
A Glimpse of the Future

Time: A few years from now, Sunday.
Place: Speakers' Corner, Hyde Park, London.
Cast: Mullahs milling about; today's crowd of women in fur coats has been replaced by women covered head-to-toe in black veils.

Hojatoleslam Hashemi-Rafsanjani climbs onto an empty Coke crate and starts addressing the crowd, who are shouting, "May Allah bless Mohammad and the descendants of Mohammad."

"Beloved congregation!" he begins. "I am calling on international public opinion and on Britain's police forces! The regime which has now usurped power in Iran must be overthrown as soon as possible." (The crowd shout: "Allah is the greatest. Allah is the greatest.") Muslims have been driven into exile, have lost their homeland and have fallen into tragic circumstances.

"Gentlemen, you have all seen the old beggar who sits on the floor at the station at Kensington High Street, trying to make a living on spare change. But do you know who he is? He is none other then Ayatollah Montazeri, the Esteemed Islamic Juriconsult. (Women in chadors cry out loud.)

"Brother Lajevardi, the former chief warden of Evin Prison who was vilified by the imperialist media and accused of torture and summary executions, has been executed at his very own jail without trial or access to a lawyer. This is an unprecedented atrocity. We call on Amnesty International and on the International Committee of the Red Cross to investigate the circumstances of brother Lajevardi's execution. And where is Imam Khomeini himself? Why doesn't Mr Qaddafi give a clear reply to this question posed by the clerical opposition abroad? I ask in the Name of God, in the name of Islam, and in the name of human rights if it is not a crime that our fundamentalist, Muslim brother Behzad Nabavi, who did so much for the Revolution should now be working as a bus conductor in Damascus? And again, where is the Imam? Where did they take him after the fall of the Islamic Republic? The present criminal and savage regime has imprisoned all Majlis deputies, except Bazargan, in the Tehran zoo and their visitors have to buy tickets to see them. We call on the international community to arrange for Mr Bazargan to be imprisoned as well."

The crowd shout in chorus:

 Khomeini, Khomeini,

 You who were our beloved Leader,

 Why did you disappear?

Rafsanjani: "We want our Imam back. And what has happened to our President? (The crowd cry.) Why should our President, our elected President Khamenei be in jail?

And not in Iran either, but in Algeria, and on charges of picking pockets? Shame on the murderers who are now ruling Iran. Curse and damnation on these blood-sucking cut-throats.

"My house has now been turned into a museum. The Imam's own residence is now a stable. In the evenings they bring a donkey out on his balcony and make him bray. In Tehran's Seyyed-Nassredin area, a devout follower of the Imam has been shot in the head while shouting 'Allah is the Greatest' from his rooftop. He was shot from a communications satellite. It's true, I'm not lying. (The crowd shout: 'Allah is the Greatest. Allah is the Greatest.')

"That outstanding preacher, brother Fakhreddin Hejazi is now in hiding in Iran. Agents of the illegitimate ruling clique want to arrest him and show him the Imam's blessed olives. I must humbly report to the beloved British Prime Minister, Mrs Shirley Williams, that our gallant sister A'zam Taleqani, a Mijlis deputy before the take-over of the country by the present blood-thirsty gang, has been arrested while trying to escape, wearing men's clothes as well as fake bread and moustache. She is now being interrogated by police agents who are not related to her in any way, either by blood or marriage, and hence have no right to question her.

"Where is our Imam? Brother Qaddafi, it is from you that we want our Imam.

"In Spain, Grand Ayatollahs Azari-Qomi, Moussavi-Ardebili and Sanei sleep in the rough. The torturers at Evin prison have shaved Ayatollah Khalkhali's beard, taken off his turban, forced him to wear a clown's garb and to appear on television's New Year entertainment.

"I call on all opposition newspapers, especially the *Mullah News*, the *Mullah Times*, the *Mullah in Exile*, the *Mullah's Messenger* and the *Mullah's Voice*, and especially brother Bani-Sadr's *Islamic Revolution*, which kept up the name of the Islamic Revolution even when he joined the opposition fighting us—I call on all these newspapers to join their voices and forces againt the illegitimate usurper regime and make sure that we don't turn into the same confused mish-mash shape as that of the previous opposition. Of course, they did manage to topple us, all the same, but then the regime now in power has nothing to do with any of them. It is neither a monarchy, nor a republic, neither a nationalist regime, nor a communist one, nor a democratic Islamic one, nor an Islamic one, nor a military one, nor anything else! Even all the foreign observers and commentators have been dumb founded by this regime, which hasn't been defined in any dictionary or encyclopaedia.

"And now the second part of the Friday Prayers service in Hyde Park. On this beloved Sunday afternoon, we pray for the souls of the martyrs of Islam, especially those who were martyred as soon as they heard the regime had been changed: the muezzin brother who leapt from the minaret; the trader brother in the bazaar who prostrated himself dur-ing his prayers and never got up again; the clergy brother who heard the news while wrapping his turban round his head and wrapped the rest of it round his neck; the parachutist brother who heard the news during a free fall and decided to stay up there between heaven and earth; and my own martyred brother Mohammad Hashemi-

Rafsanjani, head of Radio and Television, who hanged himself from the transmitter antenna at the television station. Let us salute them all.

"We shall re-establish the Islamic Republic, this time on the hallowed, green lawn of Hyde Park, and we call on brother Moammar Qaddafi to give our Imam back, otherwise we'll have to kidnap 52 Libyan terrorists and take them hostage in London.

Amen."

Editor's Note: Of course, after the fall of the mullahs' regime, this blood-thirsty, cannibal lot will have enough money in their Swiss bank accounts, and they won't have to beg. Nonetheless they're not going to stop short of such hypocritical demonstrations. So don't be surprised if some time in the future you are stopped on the street in a foreign land by, say, Commerce Minister Asgar-Owladi, who asks if you can spare a few coins so he can buy himself a Big Mac!

10 March 1984

An American Conspiracy
by Alfred Hitchcock

New York (AP)—23 May 1986—Iran's UN representative, caught allegedly stealing a raincoat from a shop, was freed because of diplomatic immunity. An Iranian spokesman accused the CIA of a "dirty trick."

The FBI had chosen a very wet day for its evil plot. Relying on the most sophisticated meteorological equipment and techniques, they had decided that May 7 was to be D-Day.

Late in the afternoon of the 6th of May, as the sun set behind New York's skyscrapers, fell at the foot of the Statue Liberty and sank into the waters of Hudson Bay, three top FBI agents, armed with hand grenades, tear-gas and daggers entered the residential apartment of the Ambassador of the Islamic Republic to the United Nations, Mr Saeed Rajaie-Khorassani. They went directly and quickly to Mr Rajaie-Khorassani's wardrobe and carefully opened its doors. One agent placed a small bomb in the pocket of Mr Rajaie-Khorassani's raincoat, which was hanging on a wire coat-hanger. Another agent took his dagger out and cut the Ambassador's overcoat into pieces and the third man grabbed the envoy's umbrella, which was innocently leaning against the wall inside the wardrobe, banged it across his thigh and snapped it in two, like a fresh cucumber.

Later in the evening, Ambassador Rajaie-Khorassani returned home after a hard day's work fighting imperialism at the UN and went straight to bed. Before going to sleep, the Imam's envoy listened, as usual, to the latest news on the radio. The weatherman was predicting a cloudburst for the next day. But the Ambassador thought: "It doesn't really matter. I've got a raincoat, an umbrella and even an overcoat." Having said that to himself, he went peacefully to sleep, not knowing that the satanic hands of international arrogance, emerging from the sleeves of world-predator imperialism, had hatched devilish plots for his morrow.

Our indefatigeable hero awakened to the sound of the heavy drumming of huge raindrops against his window pane. Morning had broken. Through the window he could see the Statue of Liberty in the distance, enduring sheets of rain over her weary body. "O Liberty," Saeed murmured through his teeth, "all this rain, and you still endure." To ensure that these words would not fade from his memory, he jotted them down immediately on a piece of paper. He whispered the sentence once again and then looked at himself in the mirror: "O Rajaie-Khorassani, what a master of words you are!" He then dated the record of his creativity: "7 May 1986 A.D., 27 Sha'aban 1406 A.H."

Ready to leave for work, Saeed went to the wardrobe

to pick up his raincoat, but the small pocket bomb had turned it into a pile of ash. He reached for his overcoat, but found it shredded into a thousand bits. And he saw his umbrella broken in two. He picked up the two umbrella halves, went over to the window and showed them to the Statue of Liberty, as if to say: "Look! These were my umbrella. You and I, it would appear, are destined for the same fate."

The spirit of the Party of Allah which filled Saeed enabled him to withstand the pressures of the moment and maintain self-control. He knew that he had been marked for assassination. He thanked God that he had not been inside his raincoat or under the umbrella when the assassins had struck. "I shall go out and endure the rain." he thought, "just like the Statue of Liberty…"

Walking in the rain without protection, the chaste Ambassador of the Islamic Republic happened to pass by the world famous New York department store, Alexander's. In the windows of the store there were piles of raincoats, and nothing but raincoats. Each one at only $99.99! What luck! "They call this a miracle," Rajaie-Khorassani thought. He thanked the Invisible 12th Imam for his good fortune and saluted Imam Khomeini too.

What Saeed did not know was that this was a trap laid by the FBI. He did not know that the FBI agents, aided and abetted by Alexander's management, had spent the whole night arranging a fake "sale" for display in the store's windows. Indeed, Alexander's was the first department store that Ambassador Rajaie-Khorassani would pass on his way to work, and the FBI mercenaries who had already destroyed his umbrella, his raincoat and his overcoat were confident that this exceptional sale, with flood-lit windows filled to the brim with raincoats, would not escape the sharp eyes of the Islamic Republic's diplomat par excellence on his way from home to the UN Headquarters.

The chaste and innocent Ambassador sought refuge from the rain under the roof of the department store and, as soon as he was inside, made his way to the raincoat racks. He did not know that on that day, there was no one working at Alexander's except agents of the FBI, the CIA and Pentagon. He was unaware that the man sitting at the cashier's desk was Richard Helms, and that the woman who pretended to be in charge of the cosmetics department was in fact a veteran CIA operative.

Totally oblivious to his situation, Rajaie-Khorassani picked up a raincoat and tried it on. No sooner had he done that than in the White House a telephone rang on President Reagan's desk.

—Ring, ring, ring!

—Hello, the President speaking.

—He's put it on, Sir!

—He's put what on?

—The raincoat, Sir!

—Great. That's great!

—Shall we catch him, Sir?

—No, you idiot! First get that price tag off the raincoat!

—Very well, Sir.

The Defence Secretary put the phone down, went to a far corner of the store and pressed a button on a remote control device. Suddenly the price tag, which was attached to Saeed's new raincoat by a plastic wire, fell mysteriously to the floor. Rajaie-Khorassani, who had decided to buy the raincoat, made his way towards the cash desk to pay the price to the very last cent.

—Ring, ring, ring.

—Hello, Ronnie speaking.

—Sir, we've lasered the price tag off the raincoat.

—Get him now!

President Reagan put the phone down and began pacing up and down the Oval Office. He then went back to his desk, picked up the blue telephone and said in a hurried voice: "Hello, it's the President here. Get me Prime Minister Thatcher on the line right away...Maggie? Hi, Ron here. It's about those F-111's we were going to fly from your place over here to bomb Rajaie-Khorassani's apartment. Well, I'm just calling to say the plan's off, because we found another way to get rid of the guy....Yeah, a very cute little conspiracy....What, What?....No, nothing like that, just a little shoplifting. We've framed him with attempting to steal a raincoat from Alexander's in New York!...You know, this sort of thing suits the Ayatollah's ambassadors much better. But thanks anyway for offering your cooperation."

24 June 1985

Describe America
An Essay by Sadeq Sedaqat

In the name of Allah, the Compassionate, the Merciful. America! America is a country with a striped flag, which looks like my uncle's pyjama trousers, and this uncle, last week, when he went out in his pyjama trousers to buy bread from the bakery was arrested by the Islamic guards who executed him on charges of cooperating with America. In his two-minute trial, my uncle defended himself for ten seconds and told them that if his pyjama trousers had been made out of the American flag, then he would have had blue and white stars on his trouser seat, whereas there were no stars on the seat of his trousers. But they did not listen to him and executed him in his pyjama trousers.

Such was the story of my uncle who had been a merchant in the bazaar and who would always overcharge his customers and send the money over to the Imam, may peace be upon him, when he was in exile in Najaf, Iraq. After the Imam's return to Iran, this same uncle still paid money to the Imam and was always ready to give his life for the Imam. But in the end he had to give his life for his pyjama trousers.

My father says my uncle was executed because he had insulted the American flag and if he had not made the flag into pyjama trousers to wear them, but instead had made a turban out of it and wrapped it round his head, then he would not have insulted the America flag and would not have been executed.

One benefit of America is the Soviet Union, for if Columbus has not discovered America, then the Soviet Union would not have been either. In the Soviet Union too, like here in the Islamic Republic, everything is rationed and the people are free and if someone thinks they are not free then they execute that someone to free him from thinking.

But in America nothing is rationed and there are no queues and the people are really free and guns are also free, like in the Islamic Republic, and there are plenty of jobs and the wages are high and, for example, according to the labour laws, a hired killer must be paid fifty thousand dollars a month and the lives of the murderers and capitalists are like in the Islamic Republic.

We therefore conclude that the Islamic Republic is similar to both the Soviet Union and America and, as the poet says:

For the East, for the West,
Islamic Republic is the best.

Another benefit of America is Britain, which is a small country and is an island and is surrounded by water and since there are too many monarchists on it, it will soon become too heavy and will sink.

In general, America is a fertile country and on the western side of it one finds California where many Persian-language newspapers grow and they are very useful

round about the New Year when we want to make a bonfire and uphold our ancient traditions.

This was an essay by me, Sadeq Sedaqat, last year of
Class 4, but this year they have purged me on charges of
cooperating with international arrogance and have not let
me register.

Amen, O Lord of Both Worlds.

McFarlane Over The Moon

Had Mr McFarlane landed on the moon, he could hardly have achieved as much fame as he did when he got off the plane in Tehran. God only knows how weightless President Reagan's envoy must have felt when he first set foot on the airport tarmac.

Apparently Mr McFarlane's visit to Tehran had been on such short notice and so unexpected that, apart from the Majlis Speaker, Mr Rafsanjani, no important official was able to receive him at the airport.

Mr Rafsanjani told our correspondent that his detailed discussions with McFarlane were meant only for him to practise the English language. He added that all the contacts he had with Americans over the past year had been made for the purpose of learning irregular verbs.

Imam Khomeini, who everynight tunes his Russian-made Vega radio into Radio Israel's Persian broadcasts, on hearing the news turned off the radio. He also protested to Rafsanjani that five years' detention had been insufficient for McFarlane.

Imam Khomeini intends to call on the UN Security Council and other international organisations to have

McFarlane extradited from the United States in order to have him serve his jail term and then be executed. Should the United States be unwilling to extradite McFarlane, it will have to hand 52 of its diplomats over to the Islamic Republic so that they can be taken hostage by the Students Following the Imam's Line.

20 January 1987

Fable

Once upon a time there was a man who committed adultery. The religious judge sentenced him to be whipped. The next day the judge was replaced, and a second adulterer was shot by firing squad.

The first adulterer was passing by. Witnessing the second man's fate, he thanked God Almighty that he had quenched his lust one day earlier. As he walked away, he could be heard to say: "Had I done it one day late, I wouldn't be here now, mate." As the great sages of the past have said: "Don't leave till tomorrow the fornication of today."

9 February 1987